Calamity-Free
CROCHET

Calamity-Free Crochet: Troubleshooting Tips and Advice for the
Savvy Needlecrafter
© 2014 by Rotovision SA

HarperCollins books may be purchased for educational, business, or
sales promotional use. For information, please e-mail the Special
Markets Department at SPsales@harpercollins.com.

Published in 2014 by:
Harper Design
An Imprint of HarperCollins*Publishers*
10 East 53rd Street
New York, NY 10022
Tel (212) 207-7000
harperdesign@harpercollins.com
www.harpercollins.com

Distributed by:
HarperCollins*Publishers*
10 East 53rd Street
New York, NY 10022

Library of Congress Control Number: 2013947320

ISBN: 978-00-6228786-1

Commissioning Editor: Isheeta Mustafi
Assitant Editor: Tamsin Richardson
Art Director: Lucy Smith
Art Editor: Jennifer Osborne
Layout: Lucy Smith and Emma Atkinson
Cover Design: Lucy Smith
Photography: Michael Wicks
Illustrations: Sarah Lawrence

Printed in China, 2013

Calamity-Free
CROCHET

Troubleshooting Tips and Advice
for the Savvy Needlecrafter

Catherine Hirst

HARPER
DESIGN
An Imprint of HarperCollins Publishers

CONTENTS

Introduction 6
Essential crochet terms 8
Pattern abbreviations 12
International terms 14
Yarn weights 15

SECTION 1
MATERIALS

CHAPTER 1
HOOKS 18
Hook types 20
Hook sizes 22

CHAPTER 2
YARNS 24
Types of yarn 26
Fiber content 28
Yarn weights 30
Yarn colors 32
Yarn substitutions 34
Pulling yarn 36
Yarn ball bands 38
Challenging yarns 40
Other materials for crocheting 42

CHAPTER 3
NOTIONS, TRIMS, AND EXTRAS 44
Measuring and cutting tools 46
Other useful tools 47
Accessories and embellishments 49
Gallery 52

SECTION 2
TECHNIQUES FROM
START TO FINISH

CHAPTER 4
BEGINNING TO CROCHET 58
How to hold the hook 60
How to hold the yarn 61
Slip knots 62
Leaving a tail 62
Foundation chain 64
How to count chains 66
Controlling tension 66

CHAPTER 5
BASIC STITCHES 68
Inserting into a chain or stitch 70
Single crochet 72
Half double crochet 74
Double crochet 76
Triple crochet 78
Taller stitches 80
Slip stitch 82
Turning chains 84
Loop stitch 86
Spike stitch 88
Around the post stitches 90

CHAPTER 6
GAUGE SWATCHES 92
What is gauge? 94
Making your own gauge swatch 96
Measuring stitch gauge 97
Measuring row gauge 98

Choosing

Working with

Adapting

Troubleshooting

CHAPTER 7
READING PATTERNS   100
Pattern terms   102
Executing pattern instructions   104
Avoiding pattern pitfalls   106
Repeats   108
Sizing and measurements   109
Adjusting sizes   110

CHAPTER 8
BASIC STITCH PATTERNS   112
Single crochet rows   114
Half double crochet rows   115
Double crochet rows   116
Shell stitch   117
Mesh stitch   118
Front/back loop rows   119
Popcorn stitch   120
Cables   122
Gallery   124

CHAPTER 9
BASIC SHAPES   128
Increasing and decreasing   130
Flat shapes   132
Three-dimensional shapes   139

CHAPTER 10
BORDERS AND EDGES   142
Borders   144
Corners   148
Buttonholes   149
Pockets   150

CHAPTER 11
ADDING TRIMS AND
EMBELLISHMENTS   152
Adding beads and sequins   154
Adding pompoms   156
Adding buttons   158
Adding cords   160
Adding fringe   162
Adding zippers   164
Adding tassels   166

CHAPTER 12
FINISHING   168
Fastening off and weaving ends   170
Blocking   172
Joining methods   174
Care and maintenance   178

RESOURCES

Online resources and trade shows   182
Patterns and supplies   183
Further reading   184
Contributor index   185
Index   186
Acknowledgments   192

Introduction

This book is designed to be your personal crochet tutor: it will teach you everything you need to know about the craft, whether you are new to it, returning after a break, or an advanced beginner who wants to improve.

Crochet, rewarding as it is, can take a while to master, and I know the frustration that comes from getting half-way through a project only to realise it's gone completely wrong. Having to go back and start again can be disheartening and so, this book aims to preempt problems rather than address them retrospectively. Troubleshooting tips show you common pitfalls and help you ensure you have the right technique to get it right the first time.

In this book, you will first become familiar with the materials needed for crochet, including an in-depth discussion of yarn, hooks, and how to substitue these if needed. There is a huge variety of materials available for purchase, and you will be primed to make smart choices when selecting items for your projects. You will then learn the techniques and stitches that are used in patterns and projects. Remember that at these early stages, it's important to be patient; while it may be tempting to rush into making your first granny square, take a step back and practice basics such as learning to hold the hook and yarn correctly first. This is harder than you think but it gets easier with practice and will be worth the time spent on it.

When choosing your first project, it is a good idea to start with small items that can be finished quickly as this will help build your confidence. Blanket squares, for instance, are a great option because they can be made individually, one at a time, and then joined together to make a larger item. This can feel like a great accomplishment as it has the ease of a small project and the satisfaction of a working on a big piece. Please see Chapter 9 for granny square and closed square patterns. Stuffed toys are also a good choice; the sphere, tube, and hourglass patterns in the same chapter are a good place to start, as they incorporate all the necessary skills to crochet in three dimensions.

It should be noted that all text is written in American stitch terms. New crocheters might be surprised to learn that there are different stitch terms used in Europe and other parts of the world. Please see pages 14–15 for more information.

Essential crochet terms to get you started

ACRYLIC
A synthetic yarn in which man-made fibers are plied together to make yarn, often imitating animal fibers.

ALPACA
Yarn made from the alpaca's coat. Warm and highly insulative, often incorporates little hairs that make its appearance fuzzy.

ANGORA
Yarn made from the angora rabbit's coat. Very fuzzy/hairy, produces a distinctive, extremely soft fabric.

BALL
A length of yarn wound into a sphere or oblong shape. Can refer to machine-wound or hand-wound balls.

BALL BAND
The wrapper on a commercially purchased ball/skein of yarn. Will include information about dye lot, suggested needle/hook size, yardage/meterage, average tension, etc.

BALL WINDER
A device that will wind yarn from a skein into a ball/cake.

BLOCKING
Using water and sometimes steam to smooth your crochet, improving its appearance, straightening edges, and opening up openwork patterns.

BOUCLÉ
Yarn in which one of multiple plies is twisted more loosely than the others, forming distinctive loops.

BULKY/CHUNKY
A thick weight of yarn, ranging from just thicker than aran all the way up to super-bulky/rug yarn.

CASHMERE
Yarn made from the cashmere goat's coat. Very luxurious, generally the most expensive yarn on the market.

CROCHET HOOK PARTS
Bowl—The area under the lip of a crochet hook.
Head—The tip of the hook, used to insert into the stitch.
Lip—The hook part of a crochet hook.
Pad—On some crochet hooks, a depression to rest the thumb.
Shank—The long part of the hook between the lip and pad.
Throat—The part of the hook just below the lip, usually smaller in circumference than the shank.

DECREASING
To subtract stitches to a crocheted piece, usually one at a time. To decrease in a pattern usually means to subtract one stitch from the existing number of stitches.

DK

A medium-weight yarn, also referred to as "light worsted." Most popular yarn weight in the Europe.

DYE LOT

The batch of dye in which a yarn is dyed. All yarn for one project should come from the same dye lot, noted on the ball band.

FOUNDATION CHAIN

A chain made at the base or bottom of a piece of crochet, generally worked into in rows.

GAUGE/TENSION

Generally refers to the specific number of stitches per a certain measurement, usually 4 in/10 cm. Can also refer to a crocheter's individual gauge (tightness) when crocheting, and also the size of hook.

GAUGE/TENSION SWATCH

A practice square made before starting a project to determine a crocheter's individual gauge. Generally measured by 4 in/10 cm.

HANK

A skein of yarn that has been looped into a figure-8 shape.

HOOK GAUGE

Also called a needle gauge, used to size crochet hooks and knitting needles.

INCREASING

To add stitches to a crocheted piece, usually one at a time. To increase in a pattern usually means to add one stitch to the existing number of stitches.

LACEWEIGHT

A very fine-weight yarn, used to make lacy items. Also referred to as thread or cobweb.

MERINO

Yarn made from the merino sheep's coat. Very soft, higher in price than other animal fibers, warm and insulative.

MOHAIR

Yarn made from the angora goat's coat. Extremely fuzzy/hairy, it can be challenging to work with, but makes fabric that is remarkably lightweight while still very warm. Often sold in laceweight.

MOTIF/MEDALLION

An individual smaller shape that is often used in multiples to create a larger piece. Motifs can be square, hexagonal, or many other shapes. Usually worked in the round.

PICOT

A small point or loop used to accent in crochet.

ESSENTIAL CROCHET TERMS

PILLING
The excess gathering of fluff on fabric or yarn, caused by the separation of the short fibers from the long.

PLIED YARN
Yarn in which individual strands are twisted together to make one larger strand. The "ply" refers to the twist.

POST
The vertical section of a stitch.

RIGHT SIDE
The front or outside of a piece of crochet, as it will be used or worn.

ROW GAUGE
The vertical gauge—the number of rows per 4 in/10 cm.

SCHEMATIC
An illustration of a finished crochet piece, often a garment, that may be included with a pattern and will give measurements of individual sections of the piece.

SINGLE-PLY
A misnomer, as single-ply yarn is made up of one individual strand, and is not plied at all.

SKEIN
A length of yarn arranged into a long loop. Must be wound into a ball before use.

SLUB
The bump of fiber found in an uneven yarn spin.

STITCH GAUGE
The horizontal gauge—the number of stitches per 4 in/10 cm.

SWIFT
A tool with an adjustable diameter, used to hold yarn while it is being wound.

TURNING CHAIN
A chain made at the beginning of a row or round, to raise the crochet up to the height of the stitch about to be worked. The number of chains made for the turning chain is determined by which stitch will be worked in the row or round.

VARIEGATED YARN
Yarn that is dyed with more than one color. This may sometimes include gradients or shades of the same color.

WEIGHT
Refers to the thickness of the strand of a yarn.

WOOL
Can refer to yarn made from several animals, most notably the sheep. Can range from soft to coarse.

WORKING LOOP
The loop on the hook at any given time.

WORKING YARN
The yarn connected to the ball.

WORSTED/ARAN
A medium-weight yarn. Most popular yarn weight in North America.

WRONG SIDE
The back or inside of a piece of crochet, as it will be used or worn.

YARN NEEDLE
A large needle with a large eye, big enough to accommodate yarn, used to weave in ends and join pieces of crochet together.

Pattern abbreviations

alt—alternate

approx—approximately

beg—begin, or beginning

bet—between

BL—back loop

BP—back post

CC—contrasting color

ch—chain

cm—centimeter

cont—continue

dc—double crochet

dc2tog—double crochet two together (decrease)

dec—decrease

dtr—double triple

FL—front loop

foll—following

FP—front post

ft—foot

g—gram

hdc—half double crochet

in—inch

inc—increase

lb—pound

lp—loop

m—meter

mm—millimeter

oz—ounce

patt—pattern

pm—place marker

prev—previous

rem—remaining

rep—repeat

rnd—round

RS—right side

sc—single crochet

sc2tog—single crochet two together (decrease)

sk—skip

sl st—slip stitch

sp—space

ss—slip stitch

st—stitch

tog—together

tr—triple

trtr—triple triple

WS—wrong side

yd—yard

yo—yarn over

International terms

CROCHET TERMS

NORTH AMERICA	UK/EUROPE/AUSTRALIA
YO (yarn over)	YRH (yarn round hook)
Worsted	Aran
SK (skip)	Miss
Gauge	Tension

STITCH CONVERSIONS

NORTH AMERICA	UK/EUROPE/AUSTRALIA
chain (ch)	chain (ch)
single crochet (sc)	double crochet (dc)
half double crochet (hdc)	half treble (htr)
double crochet (9dc)	treble (tr)
triple crochet (trc)	double treble (dtr)

MEASUREMENT CONVERSIONS

IMPERIAL	METRIC
⅛ in	3 mm
⅜ in	1 cm
1 in	2.54 cm
12 in (1ft)	30 cm
1 yd	91.44 cm
1 yd 3 in	1 m

WEIGHT CONVERSIONS

IMPERIAL	METRIC
1 oz	28 g
1 lb (16 oz)	450 g
2 lb 3 oz	1 kg (1,000 g)

Yarn weights

There is no standardized measurement system of yarn weights, and there is much variety between yarn manufacturers' references to weights. There is a general guide and reference system, however, which this yarn weight conversion chart can assist with.

STANDARDIZED YARN WEIGHT	NORTH AMERICA	UK / EUROPE	AUSTRALIA / NZ
0 LACE	Thread Cobweb Lace Light Fingering	1 ply 2 ply 3 ply	1 ply 2 ply 3 ply
1 SUPER FINE	Fingering Baby	Sock 4 ply	4 ply
2 FINE	Sport	Light DK 5 ply	5 ply
3 LIGHT	DK Light Worsted	DK 8 ply	8 ply
4 MEDIUM	Worsted Fisherman Aran	Aran 10 ply	10 ply
5 BULKY	Bulky Rug Craft	Chunky	12 ply
6 SUPER BULKY	Super Bulky Roving Polar	Super Chunky Polar	14 ply

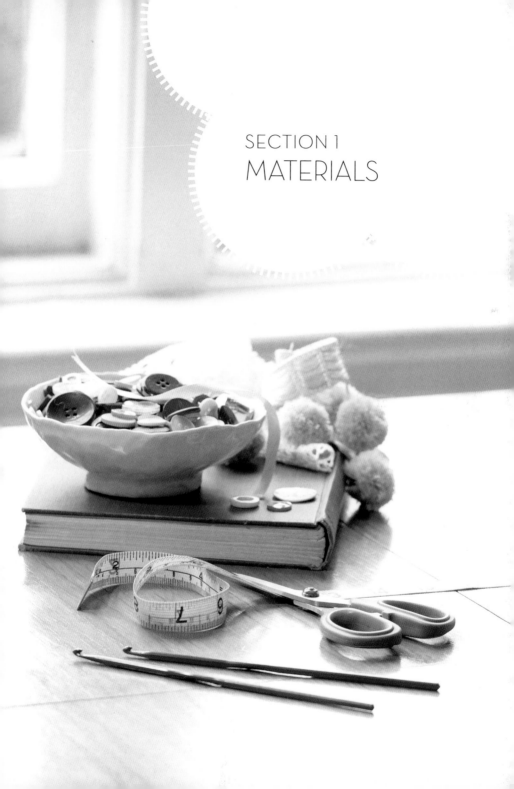

SECTION 1
MATERIALS

CHAPTER 1
Hooks

The word "crochet" means "hook" in French, and the crochet hook is the first piece of equipment you will need when starting to crochet. There is a wide variety of crochet hooks on the market, and in this chapter you will make sense of the various options, so you can choose the best hook for you.

Hook types

There are many types of crochet hook. Here is some information about the most common types available.

Regardless of the material with which your hook is made, special attention should be paid to the shape of the hook, as hooks can be very different and the shape will affect the crochet experience. The lip, or hook part of the hook, can be a soft curve or a sharp wedge shape. The shank may have a flat area to rest the thumb, or it may be a uniform tube from tip to base. The neck may be tapered or the same width as the rest of the hook, and the head, or tip, of the hook may be pointy or rounded. None of these options are right or wrong; individual crocheters should experiment with different hooks and see which one works best.

ANATOMY OF A CROCHET HOOK

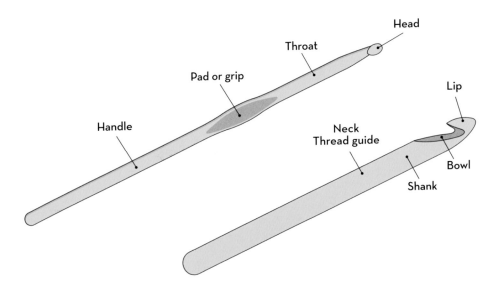

SEE ALSO

How to hold the hook: page 60

METAL

The most common material for a standard sized (between B/1 or 2.25mm and N/15 or 10.0mm) crochet hook is metal. Metal hooks have the advantage of being "fast," meaning they do not cling to the yarn like wood or bamboo hooks. Rather, they are slippery and pass through the yarn easily, making faster crochet possible. Metal hooks are easy to find and usually less expensive than wood, comparable to plastic in price. They are virtually indestructible, although crocheters with a strong grip may get some bending.

BAMBOO

Bamboo is environmentally friendly as it is a renewable resource. Bamboo hooks are less expensive than wood and are readily available. They are lighter in weight than metal and smooth in the hand. While they are flexible, they are also strong and will hold up well during years of use. Bamboo hooks will "cling" to yarn more than metal hooks, providing more control, especially when dealing with silky or novelty yarns. Some bamboo hooks have a very sharp "lip" or hook edge that can catch yarn; crocheters can use a fine-grained sandpaper to smooth that area.

STEEL

Steel is used for smaller sized crochet hooks. Generally, these tiny hooks are used to crochet thread or cotton. As the slim, hard handles can be uncomfortable during prolonged use, a comfort grip hook or added handle can be helpful.

Hook sizes

Crochet hooks come in different sizes to match up with the different thicknesses of yarns and other materials used for crochet. The size, or gauge, refers to the thickness of the shaft of the crochet hook; since you are wrapping the yarn around the hook, the thickness of the hook will affect the size of the stitch made. There are several ways these sizes are categorized—the US generally uses a lettering system, Europe, and Canada use a numbering system, and most of the rest of the world uses a gauge in millimeters.

CONVERSION CHART

LETTERING	NUMBERING	METRIC
–	14	2.00 mm
B / 1	13	2.25 mm
–	12	2.50 mm
C/2	–	2.75 mm
–	11	3.00 mm
D/3	10	3.25 mm
E/4	9	3.50 mm
F/5	–	3.75 mm
G/6	8	4.00 mm
–	–	4.25 mm
7	7	4.50 mm
H/8	6	5.00 mm
I/9	5	5.50 mm
J/10	4	6.00 mm
K/ 10$\frac{1}{2}$	3	6.50 mm
–	2	7.00 mm
L/11	0	8.00 mm
M/13	00	9.00 mm
N/15	000	10.00 mm
P/16	–	16 mm

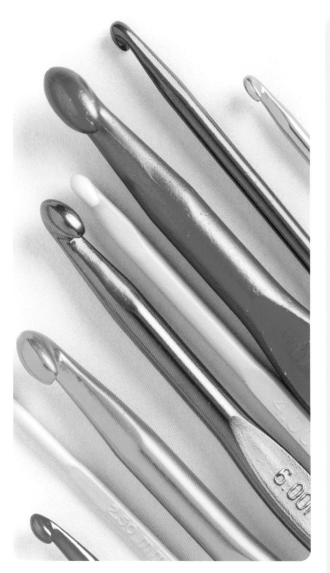

TROUBLESHOOTING

"The lip of the hook is too sharp—I am splitting my yarn with it when trying to draw through the loop."
Sometimes bamboo hooks in particular have a sharp lip. Try using an aluminum or plastic hook instead.

"I get pain in my hand after a long time crocheting."
Try using a comfort grip hook. Some hooks are sold with comfort grips already attached, or you can purchase grips to add to your existing hooks.

"I find my hook too slippery to manage."
If you are using an aluminum hook and you are having problems, try a bamboo hook—the wood will help "grip" the yarn, giving you more control. Also, be sure your hook has a depression for the thumb rest—that will help to prevent the hook from rolling more than you want it to.

▶ **SEE ALSO**
Hook types: page 20
Yarn weights: page 15

CHAPTER 2
Yarns

There is an almost inexhaustible
selection of yarn on the market,
all of which can be used to crochet.
This chapter is designed to give
you insight into the huge variety
of yarns available, and help you
decide which might be best for
your chosen project.

Types of yarn

Yarns are organized into different categories based on the way the yarn is spun when it is made.

PLIED YARN

This yarn has more than one individual strand twisted together. The name of the yarn will reflect the number of plies—2 ply, 4 ply, etc. A majority of commercially available yarn is plied, and plied yarn is used for the majority of crochet projects.

SINGLE-PLY YARN

Single-ply yarn (a misnomer, because single-ply is not plied at all) is also available. Crocheters may find single-ply yarn more difficult to work with than plied, as without the stabilizing twist of plying, the yarn can be splitty and weak, with a tendency to pill in the final product. However, single-ply yarn is perfect for felted projects, where the piece is deliberately washed in hot water with soap after completion to shrink it and make the fabric dense.

BOUCLÉ YARN

This is a type of plied yarn where one or two strands are held tight and the other is allowed to be loose, forming small loops when they are twisted together. Bouclé yarn can be difficult to work with, but it provides a striking texture that works for projects where that is desirable.

TIP

The names "2 ply" and "4 ply" can be confusing, because in the past, these names referred to a specific weight of yarn to be used with a specific hook. However, these days there is a much larger variety of yarn and a literal "2 ply" yarn could be any thickness, depending on the individual strands used. That said, "2 ply" and particularly "4 ply" are still used to refer to a specific weight of yarn, which falls into the lightweight category.

▶ **SEE ALSO**

Fiber content: page 28
Yarn weights: page 30
Yarn substitutions: page 34

Fiber content

There are three main groups of fiber content: animal fibers, plant fibers, and synthetics.

ANIMAL FIBERS

These include wool, alpaca, mohair, angora, cashmere, and silk, and are derived mainly from an animal's fleece or hair (except for silk, of course). These yarns tend to be elastic, lofty, fuzzy, and more loosely plied than plant fibers. This results in a light, insulative, and flexible fabric. Animal fiber yarns tend to be the most expensive kind, but they are desirable for garments and accessories because they breathe nicely and are very warm.

PLANT FIBERS

Fibers such as cotton, linen, flax, hemp, and rayon are derived from plants. These yarns tend to be inelastic, dense, smooth, and more tightly plied than animal fibers. This results in a dense, firm fabric. Plant fiber yarns tend to be less expensive than animal fibers, but more expensive than synthetics. They can be used for any crochet project, but are particularly well-suited to warm weather garments, home goods (such as washcloths and pot holders), and very thin lacework.

SYNTHETIC FIBERS

This group includes fibers such as acrylic, nylon, microfiber, and polyester, which are man-made and often derived from petroleum products or plastic. These yarns tend to mimic animal fibers and usually have similar qualities: elasticity, loose ply, and loftiness. However, they are not as warm or insulative as a natural animal fiber. Synthetic yarns are the least expensive, so work well for large projects such as blankets.

BLENDS

There are many fiber blend yarns on the market today: wool mixed with acrylic, cotton with bamboo, and merino with microfiber are just a few of those available. Blends can be created to make washing easier (adding a synthetic to an animal fiber can make it machine-washable), lower the price (often wool/acrylic blends are half the price of their all-wool counterparts), or combine desirable characteristics of both (in a mohair/silk blend, mohair provides fuzziness, while silk has sheen and softness). As blends can be made with disparate fiber types, there are no uniform characteristics of this group; crocheters will need to experiment with different blends to see if they suit their needs for a particular project.

▶ **SEE ALSO**

Types of yarn: page 26
Yarn substitutions: page 34

Yarn weights

The weight of a yarn refers to the thickness of the strand, and will affect the size and thickness of the finished piece, as well as the size of hook you use.

LACEWEIGHT

This is the thinnest regularly-used yarn weight. It will make a fine, drapey fabric and is well suited for lace projects where open holes will be incorporated into the stitch pattern.

LIGHTWEIGHT

Lightweight yarns include sock yarns, fingering weight, baby yarns, 2 ply, 4 ply, etc. Lightweight yarns are often used for baby projects, fine sweaters, socks, and small toys.

DOUBLE KNITTING

Often abbreviated to "DK," this medium-weight yarn is the most commonly available type of yarn in the UK and Europe, and is popular in North America as well. It creates a firmer fabric than the thinner weights and is most often used for garments, accessories, and housewares.

WORSTED/ARAN

This is the most common yarn weight available in North America It is slightly thicker than DK and is also a medium-weight yarn that can be used for almost everything. You will find the most variety of fiber types and colors in worsted-weight yarn, and the most patterns written for that yarn weight.

CHUNKY

This weight category can include anything from a yarn slightly thicker than a worsted one all the way up to one slightly thinner than a bulky or super-bulky yarn. It is often used for garments and accessories, and crochets up satisfyingly quickly. It makes a fabric that is thick, warm, and firm.

BULKY/SUPER-BULKY/RUG

This is the thickest available yarn weight. It makes a very quickly crocheted fabric and is often used for accessories or larger household items, like accent rugs.

▶ **SEE ALSO**
Hook sizes: page 22

Yarn colors

With synthetic and natural vegetable dyes being used by manufacturers, yarn is now available in every possible color and variegated colors as well.

Choosing yarn colors for a project can be a daunting task. The first consideration is, of course, personal preference, but certain colors might not be the best choice for a particular project, even if you love them. For example, doing a very complicated stitch pattern in black or another dark color will not show off the pattern to its full effect.

Highly variegated yarn will have the same problem, so a solid, lighter colored yarn will be a better choice. The texture of a yarn will also affect the color: fuzzy yarns will not show a bold color change as well as a smooth yarn; on the other hand, a softer color change line might be desired, which can be more easily achieved with a fuzzier yarn.

THE COLOR WHEEL

The color wheel is a useful tool when choosing yarns for a project. Here are three ways the wheel can be used to combine colors.

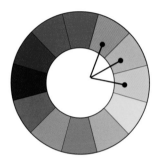

ANALOGOUS COLORS

Choosing **analogous colors** means combining up to three colors that are **next to each other** on the color wheel.

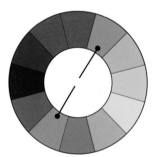

COMPLEMENTARY COLORS

Choosing **complementary colors** means combining two colors that are **opposite each other** on the color wheel.

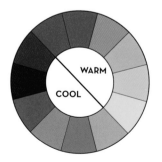

COOL- AND WARM-TONED COLORS

Choosing **cool-toned or warm-toned colors** means combining colors from only **one half of the wheel:** violet through yellow for warm tones, or green through purple for cool tones.

▶ **SEE ALSO**
Yarn weights: page 30

Yarn substitutions

Sometimes, the recommended yarn is not the best choice. It may be too expensive, or no longer available. In these and many other cases, substituting yarn is the answer. But yarns can't be simply substituted at random, as this will cause variations in the finished project.

YARN WEIGHT

Yarn comes in different weights or thicknesses. A yarn's weight will determine, in part, the size of the finished product. It will also determine, in part, the density of the fabric. So when it comes to weight, always substitute like for like to ensure the best match to the original.

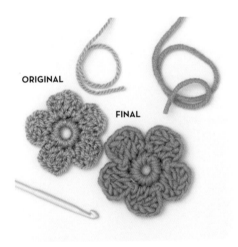

ORIGINAL

FINAL

ORIGINAL

FINAL

EXAMPLE 1
Original yarn weight: DK weight
Original hook: G/6 or 4.0 mm hook
Substituted yarn weight: Aran weight
Substituted hook: Same as original.
In this case the final piece (right) will be both larger and denser/more tightly crocheted than the original (left).

EXAMPLE 2
Original yarn weight: DK weight
Original hook: G/6 or 4.0 mm hook
Substituted yarn weight: Aran weight
Substituted hook: H/8 or 5.0 mm hook
The new piece (right) will be less dense, but will be significantly larger than the original (left).

FIBER TYPE

The type of fiber used in a yarn also affects the finished product significantly.

LAMBSWOOL

COTTON

ALPACA

SYNTHETIC

EXAMPLE 1

Original yarn weight: Lambswool
Substituted yarn weight: Cotton
The final product will be heavier, denser, and sometimes smaller than the original because plant fibers are generally more tightly twisted than animal fibers. It will not have the same insulative quality. The piece will be less elastic, which may adversely affect the shaping (around a neck hole, for example).

Original yarn weight: Cotton
Substituted yarn weight: Lambswool
In this case, because the item was designed in cotton, the elasticity of wool will not work in the crocheter's favor. The finished piece may look baggy or stretched out of shape, and if a fuzzy wool is used, stitch definition will be lost.

EXAMPLE 2

Original yarn weight: Alpaca
Substituted yarn weight: Synthetic
Substituting synthetics for animal fibers can often be successful, because most synthetic yarns are designed to mimic animal fibers. But in this case, Alpaca (like mohair, angora, and other yarns) has a fuzzy quality, and if substituting a smooth synthetic like an acrylic, the piece will not look the same as the original.

▶ **SEE ALSO**
Types of yarn: page 26
Gauge swatches: page 92

Pulling yarn

How you draw your yarn from the ball will depend on what sort of configuration the yarn is sold in, i.e., whether the yarn is a ball, skein, or hank.

BALLS

A ball of yarn is pre-wound in such a way that you can crochet with it as it is—either by pulling the end from the outside of the ball, or finding the end in the center and pulling from there. It is easier to crochet with a center-pull ball, as then the yarn does not need to unwind around the outside of the ball and the ball will stay held together. However, sometimes the center end cannot be found, and it's perfectly alright to use the outside end. Balls can be round or oblong in shape.

SKEINS AND HANKS

A skein is a long loop of yarn that is sold twisted into a long oblong called a hank. It is very important to note that you cannot crochet directly from a skein of yarn. The yarn will become knotted and be ruined. A skein of yarn must be wound into a ball before being used. You can wind a skein into a ball either by hand or with a ball winder.

▶ **SEE ALSO**
Types of yarn: page 26

WINDING A BALL BY HAND

3A

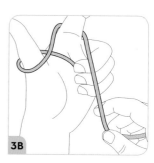

3B

4A

4B

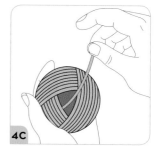

4C

1   Take any paper wrapper off the yarn and untwist into one long loop. The yarn will be held in that loop with short lengths of yarn knotted at intervals around the loop.

2   Cut each of these lengths (be careful not to cut the yarn of the loop!). One of these knots connects the two ends of the yarn. Keep close track of those ends as you don't want to lose them inside the loop.

3   To make a center-pull ball, wrap yarn around your thumb and forefinger in a figure-8 motion, always keeping the end clear of the rest of the yarn (3A, 3B).

4   When your fingers are full, take the figure-8 of yarn off and pinch the center between your thumb and forefinger, then begin winding the yarn around this center mass (4A). Continue winding the yarn, always keeping the end emerging from the center free (4B). When you have wound all the yarn, secure the end by tucking it in so it doesn't unravel. Use the end emerging from the center to crochet (4C).

WINDING WITH A BALL WINDER

Prepare the skein as per steps 1 and 2, then place it on a swift or over the back of a chair and use an automated ball winder to wind, following the instructions.

Yarn ball bands

When you purchase yarn, the ball band will give you a lot of information about it. The band will tell you what the yarn is made of, how to launder it, and often an indication of the hook size appropriate for it.

It will also give you dye lot information. A dye lot is a number that is given to yarn that was dyed in the same vat at the same time. Even if two balls of yarn are from the same manufacturer and have the same color name or number, there can be a subtle difference in color between different dye lots, a difference that will be noticeable when multiple balls are used to crochet a larger project. It is important to buy sufficient quantities of yarn all from the same dye lot to complete a project; this is one reason why estimated yarn usage is given in commercial crochet patterns. It is prudent to buy one ball more than the amount estimated for a large project (particularly a garment or large household item like a blanket) to account for discrepancies in gauge and tension and to ensure you have enough yarn of the same dye lot—otherwise, you may find the supplier no longer has the dye lot you need if you run out of yarn.

TIP

If only the knitting needle size is given on the ball band, use the same size hook as indicated for needles, in millimeters.

Some yarns are sold with the indication "no dye lot," which means the yarn is a synthetic (usually acrylic of fairly low grade) where the color can be controlled exactly. If the ball band states "no dye lot," you will not need to worry about getting all the balls you need at the same time.

▶ **SEE ALSO**

Hook sizes: page 22
Yarn weights: page 30
Yarn colors: page 32
Yarn substitutions: page 34

Pure Wool DK

28 sts

10cm/4in — 36 rows

10cm/4in

10 UK — 3 US

3¼mm

WOOLMARK

50g

In accordance with B.S.984
Approx Length 125m (136yds)

Machine Wash,
Warm Gentle

Iron Moderate
Heat

Dry Clean,
Any Solvent

Do Not
Bleach

Do Not
Tumble Dry

Dry Flat
In Shade

SH
008

LOT
9640

Made in Romania
100% WOOL
100% WOOLE
100% LAINE

Challenging yarns

BOUCLÉ

Bouclé yarn, as described on page 27, has distinctive twists and loops of yarn incorporated through the strand. It produces a highly textured fabric, and this texture is what makes it more challenging to crochet. Bouclé is not suitable for a beginner who is not yet as adept at seeing the stitches and where the hook needs to be inserted.

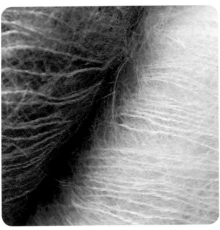

MOHAIR

Mohair is a distinctively fuzzy yarn produced from the hair of the angora goat (not to be confused with angora yarn, which is made from the coat of the angora rabbit). Like other very fuzzy yarns, such as some alpacas and angora, mohair can be challenging to crochet for the same reason as bouclé; i.e., it is difficult to see the individual stitches and to know where to insert the hook. Mohair is amazingly warm and insulative, and the fuzziness produces a beautiful "halo" around the fabric that especially suits accessories and garments.

TIP

When first working with bouclé, choose a light color as this can make it easier to see the stitches. With mohair, start with a small project where the exact size doesn't matter, so a gauge swatch is unnecessary.

NOVELTY YARNS

Yarns such as eyelash, "fun fur," metallic, and ribbon yarns are known as novelty yarns. These are typically synthetic yarns that have added texture, shine, or other effects added during the manufacturing process. Because of the uneven nature of these yarns, they can be a challenge for newer crocheters. Novelty yarns are often best used as an accent on a piece of crochet, such as an edging or stripe, rather than as the main body of the piece. They are generally inexpensive and readily available.

"SPLITTY" YARN

Unlike the other terms above, "splitty" is not a group of yarns that will be labeled as such in a shop, but splitty yarn is more difficult to work with, and thus deserves a mention. A yarn is splitty when it is loosely plied or twisted, making it easier for the crocheter to accidentally insert the hook through the body of the strand (splitting the yarn), rather than inserting under the yarn. The unworked strands left over will make your work look untidy. Splitty yarn can be identified at the time of purchase: pull out a short length of the yarn and examine it. If the yarn looks loosely plied or the plies appear straight rather than twisted together, it could well be splitty. Plant fibers are more likely to be splitty than animal fibers, because the individual strands do not cling together as well as animal fiber strands do.

▶ **SEE ALSO**
Fiber content : page 28

Other materials for crocheting

Any material that is flexible enough to wrap around a hook can be crocheted. Soft leather can be used to make bags or household goods. Paper yarn and raffia can be used to create lesser used art pieces or accessories. By crocheting with artistic wire, you can make jewelry. Fabric can be cut into strips and crocheted into a myriad of objects, including rugs, bags, and bowls/baskets.

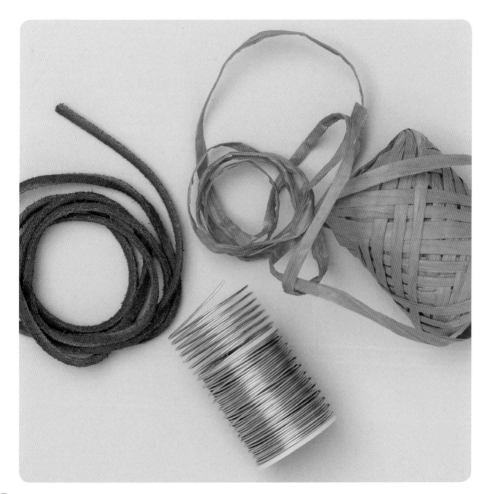

TROUBLESHOOTING

"Can I combine different types of yarn in my project?"
Sometimes, even when the same weight and fiber type is used, two yarns can crochet up very differently.

Stitch definition: A yarn that is less fuzzy and more tightly twisted, and possibly with some sheen, will have better stitch definition than another yarn. Sometimes stitch definition is not what is desired, as the final product looks better with a softer looking, more uniform fabric.

Drape: The drape of a yarn is determined by how tightly it is crocheted, and also by how stiff the original yarn is (bamboo yarn, for example, has a lot of drape). Again, sometimes drape is not desirable—a highly tailored or shaped object may be improved with a stiffer yarn that holds its shape well.

Look: Some yarns are smooth and shiny, others are muted and slubby. A handspun 100% merino will usually look very different from a machine-spun 100% merino. Color considerations also fall under this category. An original piece crocheted with soft pastels will resemble a substituted piece with bright primary colors only a little.

Feel: The feel in the hand while crocheting and the feel of the finished object will both be affected by the yarn used. Some wools are scratchy and rough, while others are buttery-soft. Acrylics and other synthetics have an incredible range of feel, from plastic, stiff, and almost squeaky, to silky and squishy.

CHAPTER 3
Notions, Trims, and Extras

Although you can crochet with just a hook and yarn, other tools will make your job easier, especially when you're following a commercial crochet pattern. Added extras like trims and buttons can make your work look more finished or add a decorative effect to a piece of plain crochet.

Measuring and cutting tools

It is important to have good quality tools to take accurate measurements of your gauge swatches and crochet in progress. Sharp scissors are also a must for crochet—get a good pair and only use them for needlecraft.

MEASURING TAPE

A measuring tape is essential for ensuring you have the right length of fabric to achieve the perfectly sized finished product, and to check your gauge/tension.

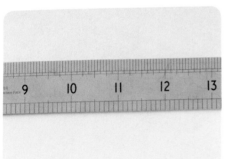

STRAIGHT RULER

A straight ruler can be helpful when measuring curling fabric or fabric that tends to shift under a measuring tape. Be careful not to compress the fabric under the ruler too much when measuring for gauge, or you will change the measurement.

SCISSORS

A nice pair of sharp scissors will help snip your yarn cleanly. Small embroidery scissors have sharp tips which help when you need to snip one piece of yarn but not another.

Other useful tools

A yarn needle (or several!) is necessary, and a hook gauge will come in handy—add them to your arsenal when you first start to crochet. Keep all your crochet tools together so they are at hand when you need them.

YARN NEEDLE

These are also known as darning needles or hand-sewing needles. A yarn needle is simply a needle with an eye that is big enough to accommodate yarn. They come with sharp or dull tips.

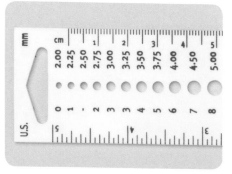

HOOK GAUGE

A hook gauge is a flat piece of plastic or wood with differently sized holes, and is used to measure crochet hooks. If you find your hook size has worn off the handle or the hook has been sized with an outdated measurement system, simply insert the hook into the holes until you find an exact match, then print the size on the hook with a permanent marker.

▶ **SEE ALSO**

Measuring row gauge: page 98
Challenging yarns: page 40
Hook sizes: page 22

OTHER USEFUL TOOLS

STITCH MARKERS

Stitch markers are used to keep track of a particular stitch, row, or side of your work. They are essential for certain crochet projects and will make things easier in others. Here are some examples of when to use stitch markers:

- When working in continuous rounds in single crochet, as opposed to working back and forth in rows, to make a three-dimensional object. It is impossible to know where the beginning of the round is without a stitch marker.
- When a pattern asks you to work a certain number of rows. You can insert the stitch marker at the beginning of the section, or at intervals so you won't need to count the individual rows over and over again.
- When a pattern asks you to keep track of which side of the work is the "right side" and which is the "wrong side." This can be difficult as most crochet fabric is reversible, but it's important to get it right when you are making garments.
- When you are working a large number of chains. You can insert a marker every 10, 20, or 50 chains, so that you won't need to count them over and over again.

There are commercial stitch markers available, but you can also use a safety pin, or a spare piece of yarn in a contrasting color. When marking a stitch just made, insert the marker under the "v" of the stitch, which will be just behind the loop on the hook.

TIP

Do not use closed-circle knitting stitch markers in crochet! You will have to cut them out afterward. You must use an openable marker.

Accessories and embellishments

Adding accessories and embellishments to crochet can really change the look of a project. Here are some of the most commonly used:

LACE

Adding a lace edge to crocheted pieces gives a pretty, feminine appeal. Lace edging is an often-seen addition to the trendy "boho-chic" look. You can add lace to garments, accessories, or soft furnishings. When choosing a lace edging, ensure the side to be attached is substantial enough to be sewn or crocheted securely to the piece.

BUTTONS

Buttons can be functional or decorative. When choosing buttons for a finished project, take the item with you to the store and hold the buttons next to the work to ensure they coordinate perfectly. If possible, slip them through the buttonholes to make sure they are the correct size. (The button should be slightly larger than the hole.) You can use two types of buttons in crochet: sew-through buttons have holes in them so they can be sewn flush to the fabric, and shaft or shank buttons have a short shank that raises the button off the surface of the fabric.

TIP

Be sure to attach buttons very securely to any item that is to be given to/used by a baby. Shaft buttons are not advised for baby items.

▶ **SEE ALSO**
Buttonholes: page 149
Adding buttons: page 158

ACCESSORIES AND EMBELLISHMENTS

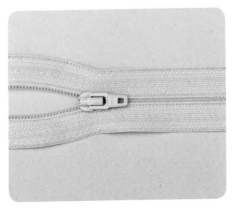

ZIPPERS

Zippers can be used in crocheted items like sweaters, cushion covers, and purses. When purchasing zippers, ensure that the zipper is slightly longer (about 1in/2cm) than the opening. There are three types of zippers. A two-way separating zipper has a pull at the top and the bottom of the zippers; a one-way separating zipper unzips and parts completely; a non-separating zipper opens all the way up, but does not separate from the other side.

SEQUINS AND BEADS

Sequins and beads can be incorporated into the item while crocheting, or sewn on after. When purchasing sequins and beads to be threaded onto yarn, consider that the hole in the sequin or bead must be big enough for the yarn (and also a needle big enough to use with the yarn) to pass through. If you choose to sew the item on afterward, then the hole only needs to be big enough to pass a normal sewing needle and thread through.

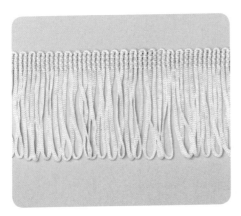

FRINGES AND TASSELS

Adding pre made fringes and tassels to your crochet will increase visual interest. They can be used as pulls on zippers for garments and handbags; to edge blankets, cushion covers, or other soft furnishings; or just to jazz up a plain project. Consider how adding the fringe or tassel will affect laundering the item though, and ensure it can be attached securely or removed before laundering.

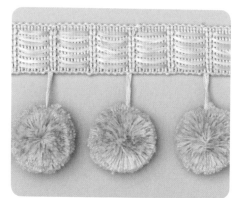

POMPOMS

Pompoms can be added to the top of a crocheted hat or the edge of a scarf, but they can also be used to embellish other crocheted items, such as pulls for a zipper, the corners of a cushion or bag, or the top of a tea or coffee pot cozy. You can buy pre made pompoms in many different sizes, colors, and fiber types.

CORDS

Cords can be used for practical reasons, such as for drawstrings in hoods or handbags, or they can be used decoratively. Pre made cords are available in a variety of materials, including hemp, leather, and wool. When choosing a cord as a drawstring, ensure the cord is long and thin enough to pass through the desired section of the work. Also ensure the ends can be knotted or otherwise secured so they do not disappear inside the piece.

▶ **SEE ALSO**

Adding zippers: page 164
Adding beads and sequins: page 154
Adding fringe: page 162

Adding tassels: page 166
Adding pompoms: page 156
Adding cords: page 160

Gallery

Opposite page:
Scarf by
Bernadette Ambergen.

This page:
Left: Striped slippers
by Şennur Öğüşlü.

Below: Reversible blanket
and baby hat set by Ashley
Jackson Rodriguez.

GALLERY

Opposite page:
Purple flower beanie
by Şennur Öğüşlü.

This page:
Left: Red gloves
by Şennur Öğüşlü.
Below: Scarves
by Şennur Öğüşlü.

SECTION 2
TECHNIQUES FROM START TO FINISH

CHAPTER 4

Beginning to Crochet

The most important skill to master when learning to crochet is how to hold the hook and yarn properly. This is crucial to succeeding with crochet. It can feel uncomfortable at first, so it is tempting to hold the hook and yarn in a more "natural" way, but that will make crocheting much more difficult. Practice your hook and yarn holds until it feels more comfortable. Once you have mastered this, you will be ready to move on to learning stitches.

How to hold the hook

You can hold the hook from above, like a knife, or from below, like a pencil. Either hold is correct, so experiment to see which hold gives you more control. You should be able to turn the hook so that the "hooky" part faces up or down. Personally, I prefer the knife hold.

Knife hold (right hand)

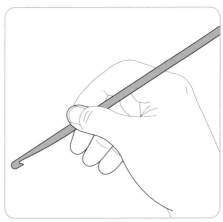

Pencil hold (right hand)

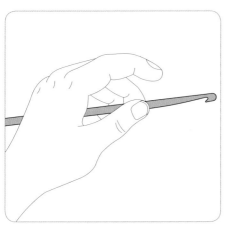

Knife hold (left hand)

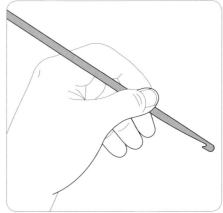

Pencil hold (left hand)

How to hold the yarn

The yarn should be tensioned so that it can be hooked and drawn through the loop on the hook without needing to pick it up and wrap it around the hook.

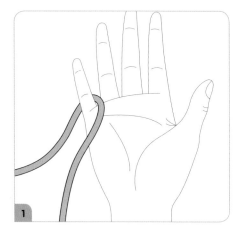

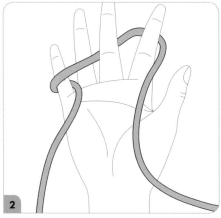

1 Take your little finger behind the strand of working yarn, scoop up the yarn, and wrap it all the way around your finger.

2 Then pass the yarn on the palm side of your ring finger, between the ring finger and middle finger, and on top (back of the hand) of both the middle finger and index finger. Either the middle finger or index finger can be raised to control the tension

▶ **SEE ALSO**
Hook types: page 20
Types of yarn: page 26

Slip knots

Most crochet projects will begin with a slip knot, an adjustable knot that is made using the technique below.

1 Make a loop of yarn.
2 Bring the working yarn behind the loop.
3 Catch the working yarn with the hook and pull a loop through.
4 Pull the tail to tighten the yarn.

Leaving a tail

When making your slip knot, leave a tail of yarn that is long enough to be woven in later.

You should leave a tail of at least 4 in/10 cm when making your slip knot. This tail will hang there until the piece is finished—do not cut it off. It will be woven in with a yarn needle later.

▶ **SEE ALSO**
How to hold the yarn: page 61
Weaving in ends: page 170

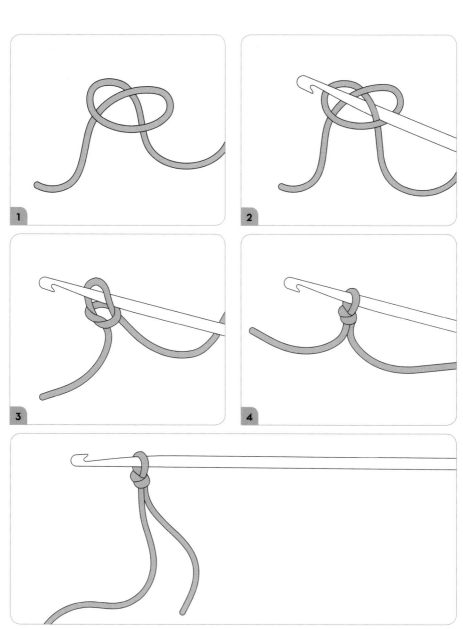

Leaving a tail

Foundation chain

The foundation chain is the bottom or base of your crochet. It is a series of loops into which you will make your crochet stitches. Learning to chain— hooking the yarn correctly to draw it through the loop on the hook—is half the battle when learning to crochet. When you have mastered the chain, you are ready to move on and learn the stitches.

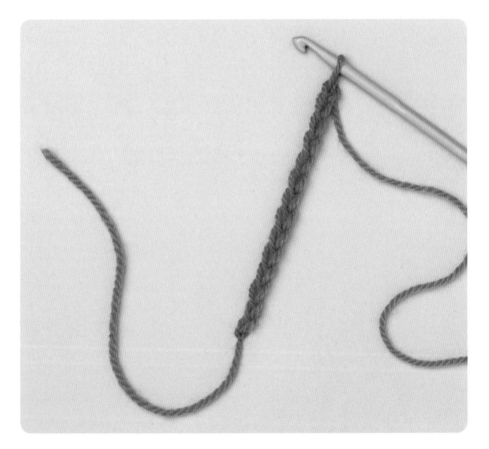

▶ **SEE ALSO**

How to hold the hook: page 60
How to hold the yarn: page 61

How to count chains: page 66
Inserting into a chain or stitch: page 70

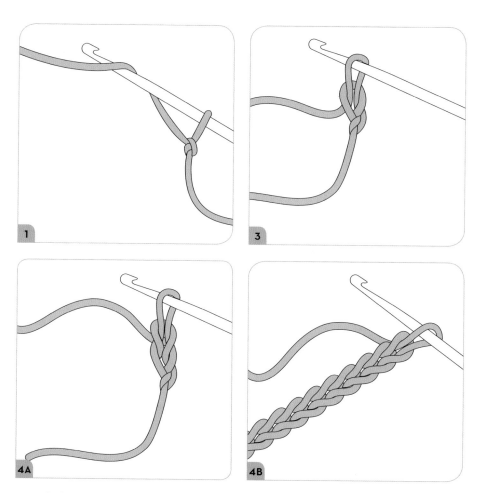

1 Push the hook forward and pass it under the working yarn to the back.

2 Turn the hook's head to catch the yarn.

3 Pull the yarn through the loop on the hook. You have now made one chain.

4 Continue pulling the yarn through the loop (4A), always moving the fingers that are holding the work up so you are holding it just under the loop on the hook.

How to count chains

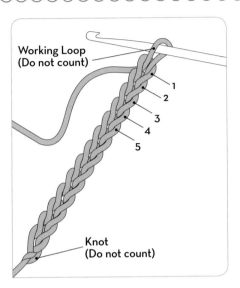

Working Loop
(Do not count)

1
2
3
4
5

Knot
(Do not count)

Look at the chain you have made. You have the loop on the hook—this is called the working loop, and never counts as a chain or a stitch. You have the knot you started with at the other end. This also does not count as a chain. Between the loop and the knot, you have a vertical line of "v"s. Each "v" is a chain. If you flip the chain over and look at the other side, you will see a line of bumps on top of the "v"s. The side with the "v"s is the front of the chain, and the side with the bumps is the back of the chain. You should work with the "v"s facing you when crocheting into the chain.

Controlling tension while making chains

TIP

There is a variation in which you crochet into the bumps on the back when working into the foundation chain—this gives a neat bottom edge. This technique can only be used for the foundation chain—do not twist your chains later in the work to work into the back.

Controlling the flow of the yarn through the hand is a skill that takes practice. The yarn should move through the hand easily enough that your work does not become too tight, but should be controlled enough to allow you to pick up the yarn and draw it through the loop on the hook without it falling off.

▶ **SEE ALSO**

Foundation chain: page 64
Inserting into a chain or stitch: page 70

TROUBLESHOOTING

"I am having trouble controlling the yarn."

There are a number of factors that affect yarn control:

1 **Fingers curled in:** If you curl your fingers into your palm, the yarn cannot flow through the hand, and your work will become too tight. Keep your fingers straight and together.

2 **Fingers splayed open:** If you allow your fingers to be too far apart, the yarn will not be controlled and it will be impossible to hook it through properly. Keep your fingers together.

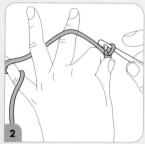

3 **Hooking yarn the wrong way:** The hook should always pass under the yarn to the back; it should never go over top of the yarn. There is no exception to this rule in crochet. If you look at your chain and see "v"s and bumps on the same side of the chain, you are wrongly picking up the yarn at intervals.

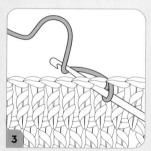

4 **Holding the work too far away from the working loop:** It is important to hold the work right underneath the working loop on the hook—this gives you the most control. The farther away from the loop you are holding your work, the less control you have and the more difficult it will be to pull the yarn and hook through the loop. This means you need to move your fingers up regularly when chaining, so you are always holding right underneath the loop.

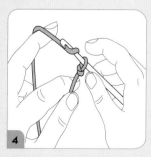

▶ **SEE ALSO**
How to hold the yarn: page 61
What is gauge?: page 94
Making your own gauge swatch: page 96

CHAPTER 5
Basic Stitches

Once you have mastered the chain stitch and have had a good deal of practice using it, it is time to learn the basic crochet stitches. In this chapter, the stitches are described using North American terms. The terms for Europe and other parts of the world are different (see page 14). Now that crochet patterns are so readily available online, it is vital to know where the pattern you are working on comes from, as not only are the stitch names different, but the same names are sometimes used for different stitches. For example, double crochet in North America and double crochet in Europe are different stitches.

Inserting into a chain or stitch

When inserting the hook into a chain or stitch, the correct technique is to insert the hook under **both legs** of the "v" of the chain or stitch. When working into the chain, some crocheters find this difficult, and will insert the hook into the middle of the "v"; this is a widely used alternative, although it will not look as neat. (The technique described on page 66 of crocheting into the bumps on the back of the foundation chain can be used as a neater alternative.)

For a stitch, it is incorrect to insert the hook under one leg of the "v" **unless the pattern is written that way**. For example, the pattern might say to crochet "into the front loop"—that is, insert your hook into the leg of the "v" closest to you. Or it might say "crochet into the back loop"—that is, insert your hook into the leg of the "v" farther away from you. Unless the pattern specifies this, you should insert your hook under both legs of the "v" of a stitch.

TIP

If you are not sure which is the next stitch, pull up gently on the hook; the stitch you have just completed will open a hole at its base and you can then advance to the next stitch along.

INSERTING INTO A STITCH
Insert the hook from front to back under both legs of the "v" of the chain or stitch.

INSERTING INTO A STITCH WORKING THROUGH THE FRONT LOOP
Insert the hook from front to back under the leg of the "v" closest to you.

INSERTING INTO A STITCH WORKING THROUGH THE BACK LOOP
Insert the hook from front to back under the leg of the "v" farther away from you.

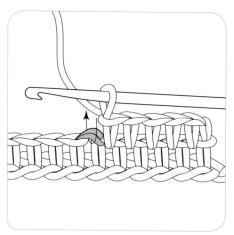

Inserting through both loops

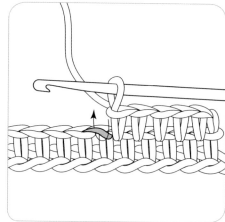

Inserting through the front loop

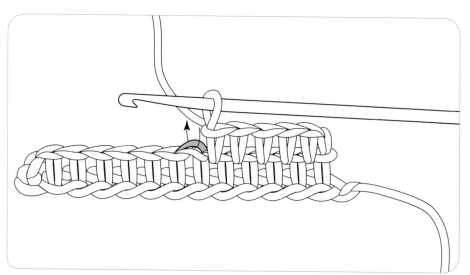

Inserting through the back loop

▶ **SEE ALSO**

Foundation chain: page 64

Single crochet

The single crochet is the shortest stitch in crochet. It is squarish—about as wide as it is tall. When worked in rows, it makes a dense, firm fabric. It is often used for toys and other projects where a tight gauge/tension is needed.

1   Insert the hook into the second chain from the hook. If you're working into a previously worked row of crochet, chain one to begin the row. This chain does not count as a stitch and should not be worked into in subsequent rows.

2   Keeping tension on the yarn, yarn over (pass the hook under the yarn to catch it; abbreviated as YO) and draw through a loop (two loops on hook).

3   YO and draw through both loops, leaving one on the hook.

4   The stitch is now complete.

5   Continue working single crochet into each chain across the row. The stitch you have just made will have made a visible hole in the chain row; do not insert back into the same chain. Move one chain to the left of the hole to make your next stitch (left-handed crocheters will move one chain to the right each stitch).

6   At the end of the row, turn the work toward you so you are ready to begin the next row, working back across the top of the stitches you have just made.

TIP

Single crochet can be difficult to count. To identify individual stitches, look for a horizontal bar of yarn across the middle of the stitch and count each one. If the work is too tight to draw the yarn through the final two loops, allow some yarn to flow through your fingers and pull gently up on the hook to loosen the loops.

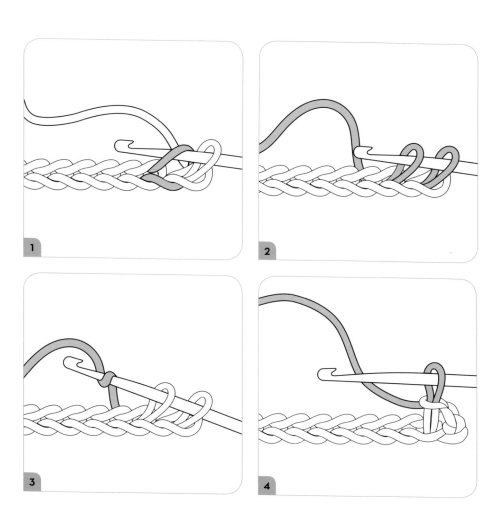

▶ SEE ALSO

How to count chains: page 66
Controlling tension while making chains: page 66
Single crochet rows: page 114

Half double crochet

The half double crochet is twice as tall as the single crochet. It produces a fabric with more drape and flexibility than single crochet, but is still solid without see-through holes. For this reason, it is often used for garments.

1 Begin the half double row by chaining two. This chain counts as the first stitch in the row and should be worked into in subsequent rows.

2 YO before inserting.

3 Insert the hook into the second stitch from the hook. If you're working into a chain, make the first half double into the third chain from the hook.

4 YO and draw through a loop (you will now have three loops on the hook).

5 YO and draw through all three loops, leaving one on the hook.

6 The stitch is now complete.

7 Continue across the row, working half double into each stitch in the row to the end. If you are working on top of a previous row of half double crochet stitches, remember to make the last stitch into the top of the chain-2 from the previous row.

8 At the end of the row, turn the work toward you so you are ready to begin the next row.

TIP

You must have a relaxed tension to be able to pull the hook through three loops at a time. If you find it difficult to draw through, allow some yarn to flow through your fingers and pull up gently on the hook to loosen the three loops before drawing the yarn and hook through.

The half double is the only crochet stitch where you draw through three loops at a time. In all other stitches, you draw through two loops at a time.

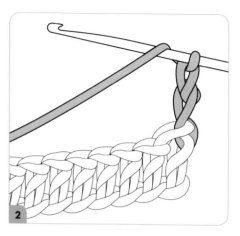

2

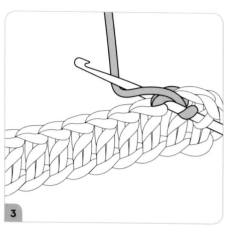

3

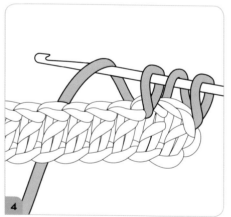

4

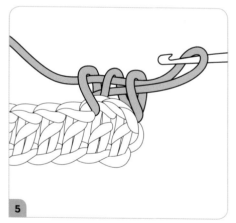

5

▶ **SEE ALSO**

Controlling tension while making chains: page 66

Half double crochet rows: page 115

Double crochet

The double crochet is the most commonly used stitch in crochet. It is taller than the half double and, depending on the yarn, is lacy enough to be see-through. It is used for granny squares, garments, accessories, and home goods.

1 Begin the double crochet row by chaining three. This chain counts as the first stitch in the row and should be worked into in subsequent rows.

2 YO before inserting the hook.

3 Insert the hook into the second stitch from the hook. If you're working into a chain, make the first double crochet into the fourth chain from the hook.

4 YO and draw through a loop (you will now have three loops on the hook).

5 YO and draw through two loops (you will now have two loops on hook)

6 YO and draw through the last two loops, leaving one on the hook.

7 The stitch is now complete.

8 Continue across the row, working double crochet into each stitch in the row to the end. If you are working on top of a previous row of double crochet stitches, remember to make the last stitch into the top of the chain-three from the previous row.

9 At the end of the row, turn the work toward you so you are ready to begin the next row.

TIP

When counting double crochet stitches, try counting the post (vertical section) of the stitch instead of the "v"s on top.

Begin by making three chains with a relaxed tension so it is easier to insert the hook on the following row to make the last stitch.

1

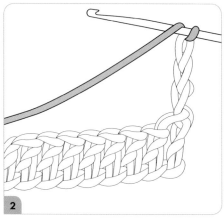

2

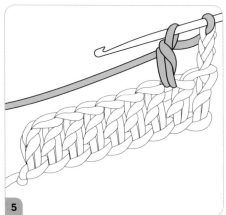

5

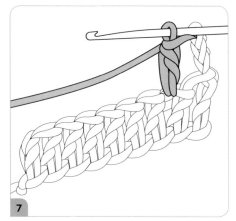

7

▶ **SEE ALSO**

How to count chains: page 66
Double crochet rows: page 116

Triple crochet

The triple crochet is a tall, openwork stitch. It has good drape and is often used in rows to make scarves, particularly ones with chunky, fuzzy yarns.

1   Begin the triple crochet row by chaining four. This chain counts as the first stitch in the row and should be worked into in subsequent rows.

2   YO twice before inserting.

3   Insert the hook into the second stitch from the hook. If you're working into a chain, make the first double crochet into the fifth chain from the hook.

4   YO and draw through a loop (you will now have four loops on the hook).

5   YO and draw through two loops (you will now have three loops on the hook).

6   YO and draw through two loops (you will now have two loops on the hook).

7   YO and draw through the last two loops, leaving only one on the hook.

8   The stitch is now complete.

9   Continue across the row, working triple crochet into each stitch in the row to the end. If you are working on top of a previous row of triple crochet stitches, remember to make the last stitch into the top of the chain-four from the previous row.

10 At the end of the row, turn the work toward you so you are ready to begin the next row.

TIP

When working triple crochet, move your fingers up so you are holding just beneath the area of the stitch currently being worked. This will allow you to have more control.

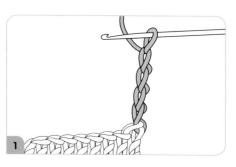
1

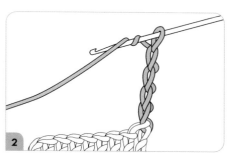
2

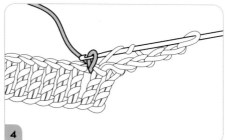
4

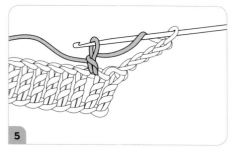
5

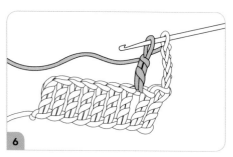
6

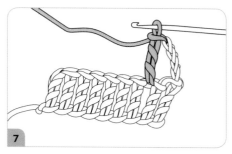
7

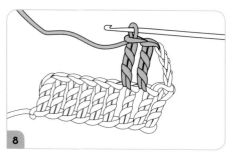
8

▶ **SEE ALSO**
Taller stitches: page 80

Taller stitches

Crochet stitches can be made taller by simply adding an additional YO before inserting into the stitch, which will make an additional YO and draw through two loops at the end of the stitch.

TRIPLE TREBLE

1   Begin the row by chaining five.

2   YO three times.

3   Insert the hook into the second stitch from the hook. If you're working into a chain, make the first double triple into the sixth chain from the hook.

4   YO and then draw through two loops, so you have four loops on your hook.

5   YO and then draw through two loops, leaving two loops on the hook.

6   YO and then draw through two loops, leaving one loop on the hook.

7   The stitch is complete.

TIP

When working taller stitches, ensure your tension is even through each step of the stitch.

Always make sure you have one loop left on the hook when a stitch is complete. If you have more than one loop, the stitch is not complete.

▶ **SEE ALSO**

Controlling tension while making chains: page 66
Triple crochet: page 78

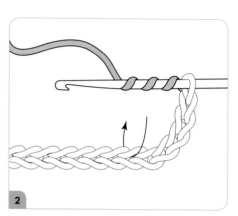

2

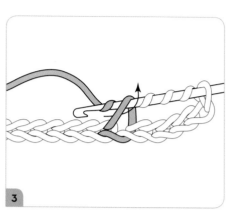

3

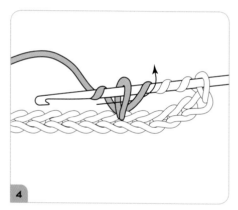

4

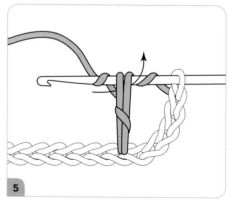

5

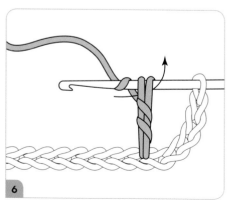

6

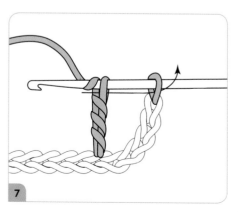

7

Slip stitch

The slip stitch is not really a stitch. It is a way to move the working loop across your work, or to close a chain loop.

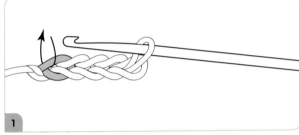

TIP

Use the slip stitch when you want to move the working loop across a row or round without creating additional height. This can eliminate the need to cut the yarn and reattach it in a different stitch or space.

If you find it difficult to draw through both the stitch and the working loop all at once, do it in two steps. **Be sure not to yarn over in between!**

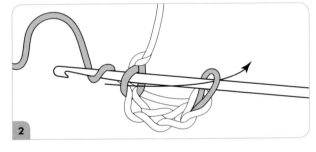

1   To make a slip stitch, insert the hook into the required stitch or chain.
2   YO and draw through both the stitch **and** the loop on the hook, without yarning over again.

▶ **SEE ALSO**
Foundation chain: page 64

TROUBLESHOOTING

"I've followed the instructions, but my stitches still don't look right!"

This could be for a variety of reasons:

1 **Gauge/tension issues:** These are usually caused by holding the hook and yarn incorrectly. Practice making chains until the yarn flows through the hand easily, then try making stitches. If your natural gauge is still very tight or very loose, compensate by using a different sized hook—a bigger hook to loosen tension or a smaller hook to tighten it.

Do not work turning chains

2 **Finding the next stitch:** It is important to accurately work one stitch into each stitch across a row. If you find it difficult to see which stitch is the next one, try looking at your work from the front, rather than the top. Pull up gently on the hook and look for a space to open up in the fabric. That space is the stitch you've just worked, so you will advance to the next stitch in the row.

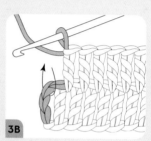

Work turning chain from row below

3 **End of the row problems:** As mentioned above, working correctly to the end of the row, including working into the turning chain from the row below, causes a lot of problems for beginners. It is important to be able to look at your work clearly. If you're not sure if you've worked each stitch to the end of the row, lay your work flat on a surface and count each stitch in the row below (by counting the vertical posts of the stitch). Then count the stitches in the row being worked. The number should be the same. If you have one fewer stitch and you do not have any obvious gaps in the middle of the row where a stitch was missed, you have probably not crocheted into the turning chain from the row below.

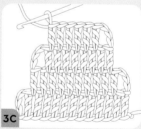

Work shrinking because turning chains have not been worked

Turning chains

At the end of a row of crochet, when you turn the work to begin the next row, you need to complete a turning chain to get to the height of the stitch you are about to work. A turning chain is a chain or series of chains that is equivalent to the height of the stitch to be worked.

Turning chains that are two chains tall or taller count as the first stitch in the row. This is because they take up space and have volume. So except for the single crochet, you will count the turning chain for all the other stitches as the first stitch, and you will crochet into the second stitch in the row. Some patterns will state this explicitly, and others will assume you are familiar with the correct technique. Please see illustrations for further information.

TIP

Because the turning chain counts as a stitch, and because you are skipping a stitch, you must crochet into the turning chain in the following row. If you do not, your work will shrink by one stitch each row. This is the most common mistake that beginner crocheters make.

TYPES OF TURNING CHAINS

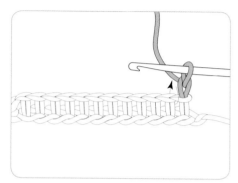

Single crochet: one chain

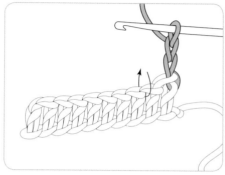

Half double crochet: two chains

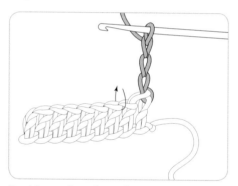

Double crochet: three chains

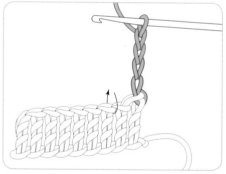

Triple crochet: four chains

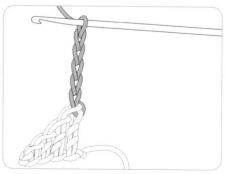

Triple treble: five chains

▶ **SEE ALSO**
Foundation chain: page 64
Inserting into a chain or stitch: page 70

Loop stitch

The loop stitch creates a looped fabric, like a rug. To achieve the loop, you hook both strands of the working yarn and pull them through. This tutorial is worked in single crochet stitch.

1   Begin by working a standard row of single crochet to the desired length. Turn the work and chain one to begin the next row.

2   Insert the hook into the first stitch. Hook both strands of the working yarn from either side of the tensioning finger and pull both through. Adjust the loop made at the back of the fabric to the desired size.

3   YO and pull through all three loops on the hook.

4   The stitch is now complete.

5   Continue working loop stitches across the row. You can make a loop on each stitch, or space the loops out between standard single crochet stitches.

6   On the following row, work standard single crochet. Alternate loop rows and standard rows.

TIP

The loop is formed on the back of the fabric, so the wrong side should be facing you when you are making the loop.

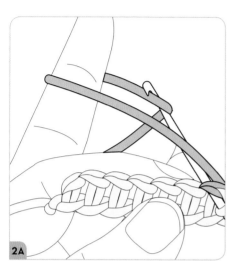

2A

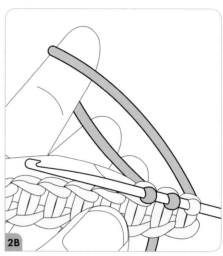

2B

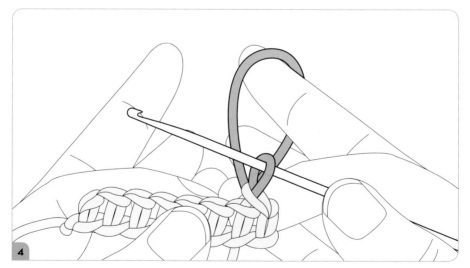

4

▶ **SEE ALSO**

Single crochet: page 72

Spike stitch

A spike stitch is worked into a row below the current one being worked. This creates a "spike" of yarn and is best shown off by being worked in a different color. This tutorial is worked in single crochet stitches, and alternating two colors of yarn, one row of each.

1   Begin by working a standard row of single crochet to the desired length in the first yarn color. Turn the work, change to the second yarn color, and chain one to begin the next row. (Alternate the colors between every row.)

2   Insert the hook into the top of the stitch below the first stitch in the current row (i.e., the first stitch of the row below the current row being worked).

3   YO and draw through, allowing enough yarn to pull through to work to the height of the current row. (You will now have two loops on the hook.)

4   YO and pull through the two loops.

5   The stitch is now complete.

6   Continue working the spike stitches across the row. You can make a spike on each stitch, or space the spike stitches out between standard single crochet stitches as in the photo shown.

TIP

If the yarn looks puckered or pulled and is not lying flat, your tension is probably too tight. Use a more relaxed tension to allow the spike to go all the way up to the height of the row being worked.

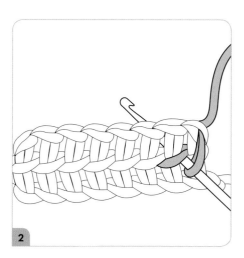

2

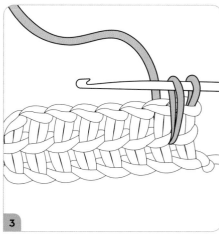

3

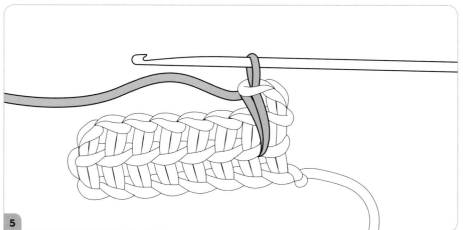

5

▶ **SEE ALSO**

Controlling tension while making chains: page 66
Double crochet: page 76

Around the post stitches

An "around the post" stitch is crocheted around the vertical part of the stitch in the row below, or a number of rows below the current row. This technique results in a highly textured, three-dimensional fabric. These stitches can be used to create ribbing, basketweave, and even cables.

There are two kinds of around the post stitches:

Back post: where the hook is held behind the work and the post of the stitch is pushed to the back.

Front post: where the hook is held in front of the work and the post of the stitch is pushed to the front.

BACK POST STITCHES

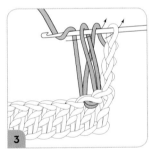

1   First work a row of standard double crochet. Turn and chain three to begin the next row.

2   Yarn over and, from the back of the work, insert the hook from back to front and back again around the post of the next stitch to be worked (pushing the post away from you).

3   Yarn over and then draw the yarn back through the post so three loops remain on the hook.

4   Finish the double crochet in the normal way: i.e., yarn over and draw through two loops twice.

FRONT POST STITCHES

This example uses double crochet stitches, but front post stitches can be made with any stitch. When working either front post or back post stitches, allow a looser tension so the yarn can be drawn back up to the height of the row being worked.

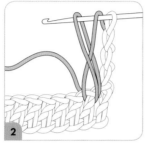
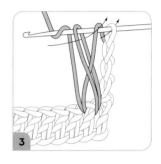

1 First work a row of standard double crochet. Turn and chain three to begin the next row.

2 Yarn over and, from the front of the work, insert hook front to back and front again around the post of the next stitch (pushing the post toward you).

3 Yarn over and then draw the yarn back through the post so three loops remain on the hook.

4 Finish the double crochet in the normal way: i.e., yarn over and draw through two loops twice.

TENSION ISSUES

You will need to experiment with tension when making an around the post stitch. If the stitch is too loose, it will bag away from the fabric and look untidy. If the stitch is too tight, it will pinch the fabric around it out of shape. In general, your tension for an around the post stitch should be slightly looser than a normal tension to allow the stitch to be worked all the way up to the height of the row being worked.

▶ **SEE ALSO**
Double crochet stitches: page 76
Basic stitch patterns: page 112

CHAPTER 6
Gauge Swatches

Many crocheters resist making gauge swatches because it is dull work and they are excited to begin their project. It's important to remember that a substantial piece of crochet, like a garment, will likely take between 20 and 100 hours of your life to make, and it is very disappointing if that piece doesn't fit after all that work. Taking an extra half hour at the beginning to ensure you have the right gauge is worth it.

What is gauge?

The gauge is the amount of tension, or tightness, with which you crochet. Each person's gauge is different and unique to them. There are two considerations regarding gauge:

Appearance of the fabric. Crocheting with a smaller hook, thicker yarn, and/or tighter tension will result in a denser fabric. Crocheting with a larger hook, thinner yarn, and/or looser tension will result in a more open fabric. Depending on the project and the desired appearance, crocheters can adjust these variables to achieve the look they want.

Size. When crocheting a piece where the exact size doesn't matter (a scarf, shawl, blanket square, bag), you can simply use the hook and yarn called for in the pattern, taking into consideration the appearance of the fabric as explained above. However, when the piece must be a particular size (a sweater, a hat, or a cushion cover to fit a particular cushion pad), then you must match the gauge called for in the pattern.

In a commercial crochet pattern, there will be a gauge/tension note at the beginning. This note might read:
20 sts and 12 rows to 4 in/10 cm over double crochet using a G/6 or 4.0 mm hook or size needed to obtain gauge.

This note means that within your fabric, you should have 20 stitches across (stitch tension) and 12 rows vertically (row tension) per 4 in/10 cm of fabric. The way to find out whether your gauge matches the gauge called for in the pattern is to make a gauge swatch.

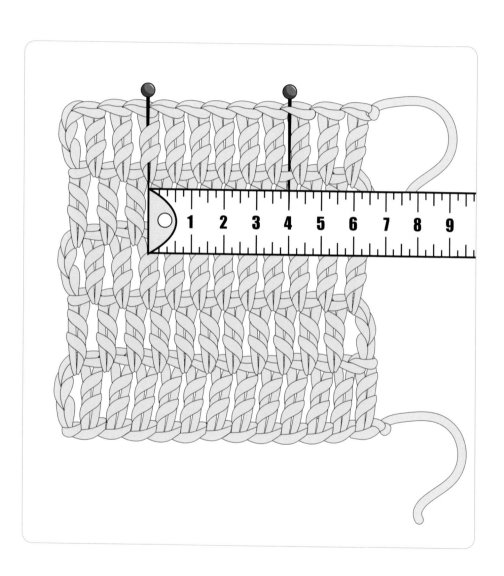

▶ **SEE ALSO**

Hook sizes: page 22
Yarn weights: page 30
Controlling tension while making chains: page 66

Making your own gauge swatch

Follow the steps below to make a swatch to determine your gauge.

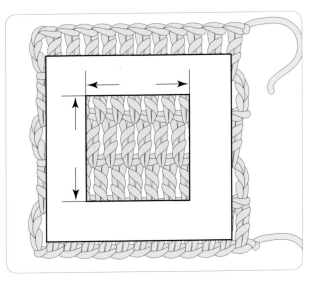

TIP

Start with the hook size used in the pattern. You can adjust the hook size after you have measured your swatch, if necessary. Work enough rows to relax your tension and allow you to begin to crochet in your normal rhythm. You may find your gauge is slightly different at the beginning and end of your swatch—most people's gauge gets looser the longer they crochet.

1 Make a chain that is slightly larger than the amount you are to measure. For example, in order to make a piece that is likely to be bigger than the sample used on page 95, start with more than 20 chains—perhaps 24 or 26 chains, plus three chains extra to serve as the initial turning chain.

2 Work the rows of stitch pattern used in your pattern. For example, in our sample piece, the swatch is to be made in double crochet rows.

3 Continue working until the vertical measurement is larger than 4 in/10 cm.

4 Place the swatch on a flat surface and have two straight pins on hand.

▶ **SEE ALSO**

Hook sizes: page 22

Measuring stitch gauge

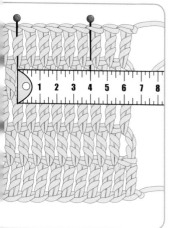

Stitch gauge is the horizontal measurement—the number of stitches per measured length.

1 Working a short distance in from the left edge of the swatch, place a pin vertically to the left of one stitch.

2 Without stretching the fabric, measure across 4 in/10 cm with a measuring tape, and place another pin vertically.

3 Carefully count the number of stitches between the pins. This number is your stitch gauge.

4 Be sure to count any half stitches within the measurement.

TIP

Work in good light, particularly when measuring fuzzy or very dark yarns. Do not stretch the fabric, unless the fabric should be slightly stretched in the final piece (for example, the brim of a hat).

Note: Stitch gauge is usually more important than row gauge. Generally speaking, the stitch gauge will determine the width (and therefore the size) of a piece, and the row gauge will only determine how long something is, which is less important in a pattern because the pattern will usually say "work until piece measures 8 in/20 cm" instead of "work another 15 rows." If you are matching the stitch gauge and not the row gauge, that is generally sufficient.

 SEE ALSO
Measuring row gauge: page 98

Measuring row gauge

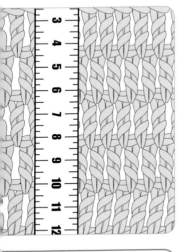

Row gauge is the vertical measurement, or, in other words, the number of rows per length.

1 Working a short distance up from the bottom edge of the swatch, place a pin horizontally below one row.

2 Without stretching the fabric, measure up 4 in/10 cm with a measuring tape, and place another pin horizontally.

3 Carefully count the number of rows between the pins. This number is your row gauge.

4 Be sure to count any half rows within the measurement.

TIP

Usually you will change hook size by one size at a time. So if you started with a G/6 or 4.0 mm hook and your stitches were too small, make another swatch with a 7 or 4.5 mm hook and compare the results.

HERE'S HOW TO DECIPHER THE RESULTS

1 Compare your results with the stated gauge for the pattern.

2 If you have more stitches per 4 in/10 cm than the stated number, your stitches are too small. Use a larger hook.

3 If you have fewer stitches per 4 in/10 cm than the stated number, your stitches are too big. Use a smaller hook.

▶ SEE ALSO

Hook sizes: page 22
Measuring stitch gauge:
page 97

TROUBLESHOOTING

"I made a gauge swatch but the size of the finished piece was still wrong."

There are a number of things that can affect your gauge swatch:

1 **Not making the gauge swatch big enough.** Because making a gauge swatch is boring and most people just want to get started on their project, they often will work only a few rows of crochet and measure that. This will not result in an accurate measurement. The crochet will not lie as flat as it would have if more rows had been worked, and the measurement may also be affected by the relative tightness of the foundation chain. Make a generous gauge swatch and measure right in the middle of the square, away from all the edges.

2 **Not using the same stitch pattern as project.** If you make your gauge swatch in rows of single crochet, and the stitch pattern of the actual piece is double crochet shells, the measurement will not relate accurately to the piece being made. Always do your gauge swatch in the same stitch pattern as the project.

3 **Not counting half stitches.** Often, when measuring the swatch, you may notice a half stitch within the measurement of 4 in/10 cm, but you might not count it because "it's only half a stitch." But remember that the gauge swatch is only a representative sample of the hundreds or thousands of stitches that will make up the final project. Multiply that half a stitch by the many lengths of 4 in/10 cm in your finished piece and you will see what a difference a half stitch can make. Be as accurate as possible with measuring the gauge swatch and you are far more likely to create a crochet piece that is the exact size you want it to be.

CHAPTER 7
Reading Patterns

When you're a beginner, reading crochet patterns can be a daunting prospect. But with practice, patterns will become as easy to read as a child's book. Understanding the terminology and instructions will help to decode a crochet pattern's meaning. Beginner crocheters should also familiarize themselves with commonly used abbreviations, listed on page 12.

Pattern terms

There is terminology that is used in most crochet patterns, and terminology that is specific to particular patterns. Here is a list of the more commonly used terms:

Bobble: A number of unfinished stitches worked into the same stitch from the round or row below, joined together at the top.

Cluster: A number of unfinished stitches worked into consecutive different stitches from the round or row below, joined together at the top.

Even/straight: To work without increasing or decreasing; i.e., to maintain the current number of stitches by working one stitch into each stitch from the round or row below.

Fasten off: To finish a piece of crochet. Cut the yarn, leaving a tail of at least 4 in/10 cm. YO with the tail just made and pull the tail all the way through the last loop to close. (See page 170.)

Foundation chain: The beginning chain at the bottom or base of a piece of crochet.

Popcorn stitch: A number of finished stitches worked into the same stitch from the round or row below, joined together at the top.

Right side/wrong side (RS/WS): The right side is the side of the work facing out in a finished piece of crochet. The wrong side is the side facing in. Most crochet fabric is reversible, but some pieces have a right side and wrong side because of the shaping that is incorporated in them (as in garments, for example).

Shell: A number of stitches worked into the same stitch or space.

Skip: This means that you do not work into the stitch or space specified.

Turning chain: A chain worked at the beginning of a round or row to bring the work up to the height of the round or row about to be worked; the number of chains worked in a turning chain depends on the stitch about to be worked in the following row. (See page 84.)

▶ **SEE ALSO**
International terms: page 14

Executing pattern instructions

Learning to read crochet patterns is easier if you understand the terminology and conventions involved. Below is the pattern for the granny square found on page 133, with annotations to help you understand how patterns are written. Following the pattern with the annotations and then without will help you feel more confident tackling crochet patterns on your own.

1   **Ch 4, ss in 1st ch to form loop.** This means to insert the hook into the first chain you made; i.e., the chain that is farthest from the hook. Make a slip stitch.

2   **Ch 3, 2 dc in loop.** In this case, you are working into the middle of the loop you have made. Insert your hook into the center of the circle. Do not insert into any of the chains. *** Ch 2, 3 dc in loop; rep from**

* twice more, ch 2, ss in top of first ch-3 to join. Fasten off. Without the repeat, this full round would read: "Ch 3, 2 dc in loop. Ch 2, 3 dc in loop. Ch 2, 3 dc in loop. Ch 2, 3 dc in loop. Ch 2, ss in top of first ch-3 to join."

3   Join new color in any ch-2 corner space.
When a pattern refers to working into a
"space," that means to insert your hook
into the space or hole formed by a number
of chains from the previous round or row.
You should not insert into a chain; rather,
insert the hook into the space below the
chain. **Ch 3, work (2 dc, ch 2, 3 dc) in
same sp as joining.** The section with
parentheses denotes that all of the stitches
and chains listed are worked into the same
space. * Ch 1, work (3 dc, ch 2, 3 dc) in
next corner sp; rep from * twice more, ch
1, ss in top of first ch-3 to join. Fasten off.

4   **Join new color in any ch-2 corner space.
Ch 3, work (2 dc, ch 2, 3 dc) in same sp as
joining. * Ch 1, 3 dc in next sp, ch 1, work (3
dc, ch 2, 3 dc) in next corner sp; rep from
* twice more, ch 1, 3 dc in next sp, ch 1,
ss in top of first ch-3 to join. Fasten off.**
Use the technique described in step 3.

5   **Join new color in any ch-2 cornerspace.
Ch 3, work (2 dc, ch 2, 3 dc) in same sp as
joining. * (Ch 1, 3 dc in next sp) twice, ch 1,
work (3 dc, ch 2, 3 dc) in next corner sp;
rep from * twice more, (ch 1, 3 dc in next
sp) twice, ch 1, ss in top of first ch-3 to join.
Fasten off.** In this round, you have both a
repeat designated using parentheses within
a repeat designated with an asterisk.
Without the repeats, this round would
read: "Ch 3, work (2 dc, ch 2, 3 dc) in
same sp as joining. Ch 1, 3 dc in next sp.
Ch 1, 3 dc in next sp. Ch 1, work (3 dc,
2 ch, 3 dc) in next corner space. Ch 1, 3
dc in next sp. Ch 1, 3 dc in next sp. Ch 1,

work (3 dc, 2 ch, 3 dc) in next corner
space. Ch 1, 3 dc in next sp. Ch 1, 3 dc in
next sp. Ch 1, work (3 dc, 2 ch, 3 dc) in
next corner space. Ch 1, 3 dc in next sp.
Ch 1, 3 dc in next sp. Ch 1, ss in top of
first ch-3 to join."

6   **Join new color in any ch-2 corner space.
Ch 3, work (2 dc, ch 2, 3 dc) in same sp as
joining. * (Ch 1, 3 dc in next sp) 3x, ch 1, ch 1,
work (3 dc, ch 2, 3 dc) in next corner sp;
rep from * twice more, (ch 1, 3 dc in next
sp) 3x, ch 1, ss in top of first ch-3 to join.
Fasten off.** Use the technique described
in step 5.

7   **Continue in this manner, always working
(3dc, ch 2, 3 dc) in corner spaces, 3 dc in
side spaces, and ch 1 to move from space
to space, until you reach the desired size.**
This instruction is given so you can make
your granny square bigger without having
each round written out. The information
you need to make your granny square
bigger is given: what to work in the corner
spaces, what to work in the side spaces,
and what to work in between.

▶ **SEE ALSO**

Pattern abbreviations: page 12

Avoiding pattern pitfalls

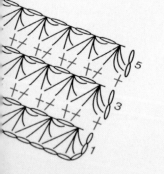

TROUBLESHOOTING

1 **"The pattern repeat does not begin at the beginning of the row/round."** This potential problem is best explained with an example: **Row 1: Ch 3, 2 dc in same st. * Ch 1, skip 1 sts, 3 dc in next st; rep from * to end of row.** In this example, there is a section of instructions that is worked only once, then the asterisk, and then the repeated instructions. When the "rep from *" is reached, the crocheter should go back only to the first asterisk and repeat from "Ch 1," **not** from the beginning of the row.

2 **"What is the difference between '4x vs 3x more'?"** Sometimes pattern repeats can be difficult to interpret. For example, if you have a pattern instruction that reads **(ch 2, 3 dc in next sp) 4x, that is the same** as an instruction that reads **(ch 2, 3 dc in next sp), rep 3x more.** In both examples, you would work the section in parentheses four times in total. Both of these examples are correct and clear conventions for writing repeats. Unfortunately, sometimes you will see a third option: **(ch 2, 3 dc in next sp) rep 4x.** This could be interpreted in two different ways: either work the section in parentheses four times in total, or take the term "rep" at face value and assume the pattern writer means to work the section five times in total. In this case, the crocheter may need to try both options to see which looks more correct. It may help to count the total number of stitches in the row, round, or section and see which interpretation would fit the number of stitches available.

3 **"The pattern is so complex, can I just read a bit at a time?"** Beginner crocheters especially may fall into this trap. Because reading and understanding a pattern can be so daunting, a beginner might break it down into smaller chunks or sections to avoid being overwhelmed. But some pattern instructions may need to be worked concurrently. For example: **Continue to work raglan decrease over next 8 rows. At the same time, decrease one stitch at neck edge on every 4th row.** In this example, a decrease is being worked at the arm edge of the front of a sweater to shape the armhole. At the same time, a decrease should be made to give shape to the neck. If you only read the first sentence of this instruction and complete the raglan decrease over 8 rows and then go back to read the next section, you will have redo some of your work in order to incorporate the neck decreases. Always read a pattern thoroughly before beginning, highlight any areas that look like potential problems or instructions that may be forgotten or missed later on.

4 **"I'm getting lost in a pattern!"** It is easy, particularly in a long and/or complex pattern, to lose your place and either erroneously repeat sections already finished or skip ahead to other sections before completing the previous work. To avoid this problem, use a method of keeping track of your place in a pattern. Self-adhesive notes work well, as they can be moved up and down the pattern and will not obscure previous pattern sections the way crossing-out will. You can also check off or highlight sections already completed. Note: be cautious when permanently obscuring previous instructions, as they may need to be repeated later.

Repeats

Repeats (as well as abbreviations) in patterns are used to save space. If crochet patterns had to be written out in full without utilizing repeats, they would be many pages long and it would be easy to get lost in the instructions. Pattern repeats are written with a number of conventions that vary from pattern to pattern. Here are a few examples of the way repeats might be written:

1 **With an asterisk.** The asterisk comes at the beginning of the section to be repeated, and is then referred to later. Example: * 1 sc in next sc, 2 sc in next sc; rep from * to end.

2 **With parentheses.** The section within the parentheses is to be repeated the number of times noted after the parentheses. Example: (Ch 1, 3 dc in next st) 3x.

3 **With square brackets.** Often used in conjunction with another repeat convention, square brackets are sometimes used the way parentheses are used as noted above. Example: * Ch 1, 3 dc in next dc, [Ch 2, skip 1 st, dc in next st] 3x, ch 1, 3 dc in next dc; rep from * to end of row. Note: square brackets are also often used to denote sizes in patterns.

Because of the prevalence of free and paid crochet patterns offered on the Internet, there are now many "amateur" crochet pattern writers, and even more repeat conventions have been utilized as a result. Single and double dashes (- and --), arrows, and double slashes (//) are all currently being used.

▶ **SEE ALSO**
Pattern abbreviations: page 12
Executing pattern instructions: page 104

Sizing and measurements

Sizes will often be denoted using square brackets and will refer back to a size guideline at the beginning of the pattern.

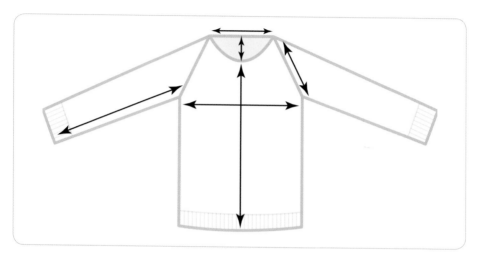

The guideline might read, "To fit XS [S, M, L]" and the pattern will have corresponding measurements per size. In the pattern itself, the instructions for each size will be written as the guideline is. Example: "Ch 100 [110, 120, 130] for foundation row." If you were making the Extra Small size, you would chain 100, the Small size 110, and so on. You will only follow the numbers for your size and ignore all the others. It is a good idea to circle or highlight your size throughout the pattern so you do not accidentally use another size's instructions. If you do not own the book/ magazine in which the pattern appears and do not wish to write in it, you can photocopy the pattern.

At the beginning of a garment pattern, there may be a schematic showing the measurements at several points of the garment. Common measurements given for a sweater include the bottom hem edge length across; the bottom hem edge to the armpit; across the shoulders; and the arm length. These measurements can be used to ensure the correct gauge/tension is achieved and the final piece will be the right size. The schematic can also be used to block the piece to the correct size.

▶ **SEE ALSO**

Adjusting sizes: page 110
Blocking: page 172

Adjusting sizes

Crochet patterns for garments can be adjusted to achieve the perfect size. Here are some examples of when and how to customize a pattern to fit:

1 Shortening or lengthening torso length, arm length, length of a skirt, finger length for gloves, slouchiness of a hat, foot length of a sock, etc: work additional or fewer even rounds/rows to desired length. Work these rounds/rows at a section where there is no increasing or decreasing. This sort of customizing can be achieved by any crocheter, including beginners.

2 Adjusting shaping: Crochet garments can be customized to accommodate narrower or wider hips, a thinner/thicker waistline, broad or narrow shoulders, etc. This sort of shaping adjustment should be attempted by more experienced crocheters who are confident making the basic stitches and with following patterns as they are written. Care should be taken to gradually increase or decrease in these areas; you can use math to work out a smooth increase or decrease that will not be visible, but will achieve the fit you want.

Here's an example: You wish to add 2 in/5 cm of additional circumference to a bust line without changing any other shaping elements of a sweater. If you simply increase until the desired circumference is reached, the body of the sweater will be longer than the size given in the pattern. Try this method instead:

1 Measure your gauge swatch to determine how many stitches you are getting per inch.

2 Take note of how many stitches the pattern as written is increasing from waist to bustline, and in how many rows/inches the increase is occurring.

3 Work out how many additional increases you will need to make to achieve your desired bust line circumference. Incorporate these increases evenly into the number of rows/inches to be worked as noted in step 2.

4 Measure before and after the increase is worked to ensure you get the correct size.

▶ **SEE ALSO**
Gauge swatches: page 92
Sizing and measurements: page 109

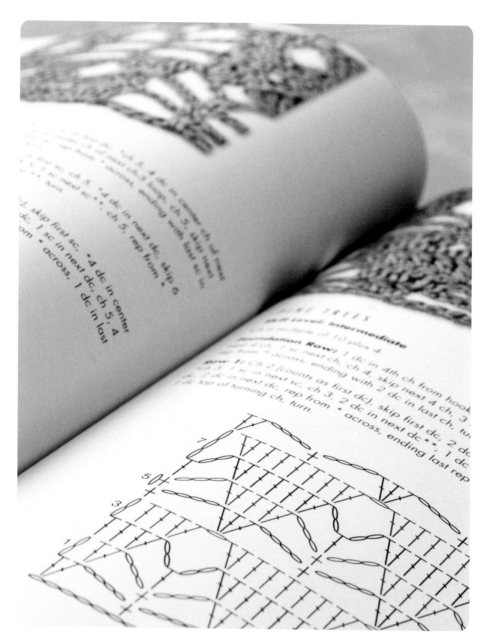

... last sc, ch 5, 4 dc in next dc, rep ...
... rep from * ... next ch, ch 3 dc ...
... from * across, ending with last sc. In
... 1 sc in next sc **, ch 5, rep from *,
... *, turn.

..., skip first sc. *4 dc in center
... dc, 1 sc in next dc, ch 5, 4
from * across, 1 dc in last

PINE TREES

Skill Level: **Intermediate**

... a multiple of 10 plus 4

Foundation Row: 1 dc in 4th ch from hook
... ch, 1 sc in next ch, ch 4, skip next 4 ch, 3
... from * across, ending with 2 dc in last dc, tur

Row 1: Ch 2 (counts as first dc), 1 sc in next dc, skip next dc **, ch 3, 1 sc in next dc, ch 3, 2 dc in next dc, rep from * across, ending last rep
... , 2 dc in next dc **, 1 dc
... 1 dc in top of turning ch, turn.

CHAPTER 8
Basic Stitch Patterns

A stitch pattern refers to the appearance of the fabric created by the stitch or combination of stitches used. The simplest stitch patterns are just individual stitches, worked in rows. Combining different stitches in the same row results in more elaborate patterns.

Single crochet rows

Single crochet fabric is firm and dense. It works particularly well in any project where you desire a firm, warm, solid fabric.

To make single crochet fabric, work chains to the desired width, and then work one chain more for a turning chain. Skip the first chain, then make a single crochet into each chain to the end. Turn the work.

Next row: Ch 1, sc into each sc to end. Turn the work.

Repeat the last row to form the pattern.

▶ **SEE ALSO**
Single crochet: page 72

Half double crochet rows

Half double crochet fabric is solid, but has more drape than single crochet. It works well for garments.

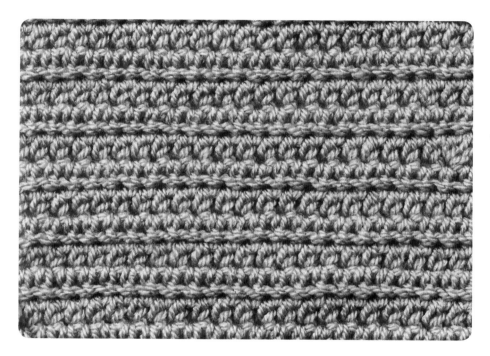

To make half double crochet fabric, work the chains to the desired width, and then add two chains more for a turning chain. Skip the first two chains, then make half double crochet into each chain to end. Turn the work.

Next row: Ch 2, skip 1st st, hdc in each hdc to end, making sure to work last st into turning chain from row below. Turn the work.

Repeat the last row to form the pattern.

 SEE ALSO
Half double crochet: page 74

Double crochet rows

Double crochet fabric is more open and you will generally be able to see through it (depending on the yarn used and your gauge).

TIP

If the fabric appears to be shrinking when you're working half double or double crochet rows, it may be that you are not working into the turning chain at the end of the row. Count your stitches carefully at the end of each row and correct any mistakes.

To make double crochet fabric, work the chains to the desired width, and then make three chains more for a turning chain. Skip the first three chains, then make double crochet into each chain to end. Turn the work.

Next row: Ch 3, skip 1st st, dc in each dc to end, making sure to work last st into turning chain from row below. Turn the work.

Repeat the last row to form the pattern.

▶ **SEE ALSO**
Double crochet: page 76

Shell stitch

Shell stitch can be worked in rows, as in the example below, and it can also be used as an edging, as on page 145. It makes a pretty, openwork fabric.

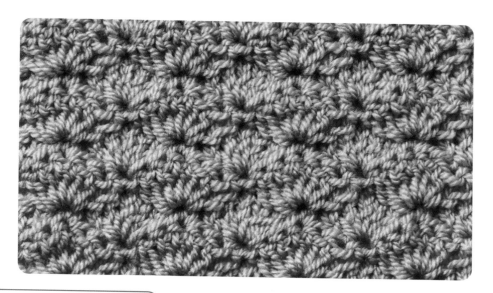

TIP

The shell of five double crochet should always be worked into the single crochet from the row below, and the single crochet should always be worked into the third of five double crochet of the shell from the row below.

To make shell stitch fabric, work any multiple of six + two chains, for example, 14, 20, or 26.

First row: Sc in 2nd ch from hook, * Skip 2 chs, 5 dc in next ch, skip 2 chs, sc in next ch; rep from * to end. Turn.

Next row: Ch 3, work 2 dc in same st. * Sc in 3rd of 5 dc of shell, work 5 dc into next sc; rep from * to end, work 3 dc in last sc. Turn.

Next row: Ch 1, sc in same st. * 5 dc in next sc, sc in 3rd of 5 dc of shell; rep from * to end, sc in top of turning ch from previous row.

Repeat last two rows to form the pattern.

▶ **SEE ALSO**
Borders: page 144

Mesh stitch

Mesh stitch makes an open, grid-like fabric. It can be used to nice effect in shawls and other lacy items.

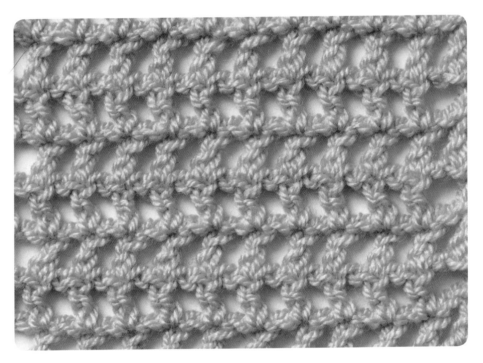

To make mesh stitch fabric, work the chains to the desired width, then make four chains (these four chains count as the three-chain turning chain plus one chain). Skip 4 chs, dc in next ch. * Ch 1, skip 1 ch, dc in next ch; rep from * to end. Turn.

Next row: Ch 4, dc in next dc. * Ch 1, dc in next dc; rep from * to end, working last dc into turning ch from row below. Turn.

Repeat the last row to form the pattern.

▶ **SEE ALSO**
Double crochet: page 76

Front/back loop rows

Working into the front or back loop of a stitch creates a ridge on one side of the work that has a different appearance than traditionally worked crochet. It will also make the fabric more stretchy and pliable.

Work as instructed for the stitch desired as above, but insert the hook only into the front loop or back loop of the stitch.

▶ **SEE ALSO**
Single crochet: page 72

Popcorn stitch

Popcorn stitch is a highly textured, three-dimensional stitch pattern that works well in decorative items such as tea cozies and pot holders, as well as accessories like scarves.

TIP

A front popcorn will protrude from the side of the work facing you, while a back popcorn will push out on the other side. You should work front popcorn with the right side facing, and back popcorn with the wrong side facing.

You will go through yarn quickly when making popcorn stitch. Ensure you have ample yarn in the same dye lot to finish the project. To make popcorn stitch, work any odd number of chains to the desired width, then four chains more for a turning chain. Dc in 4th ch from hook and in each ch to end. Turn.

Next row: Ch 3, * work back popcorn as follows: (5 dc in next st, take hook out of working loop, insert back to front into the 1st of the 5 dc and back through working loop, YO and pull through loop and st), tr in next st; rep from * to end. Turn.

Next row: Ch 3, * work front popcorn as follows: (5 dc in next st, take hook out of working loop, insert front to back into the 1st of the 5dc and back through working loop, YO and pull through loop and st), dc in next st, rep from * to end. Turn. Repeat last two rows to form pattern.

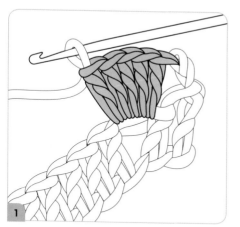

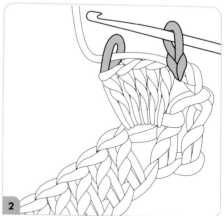

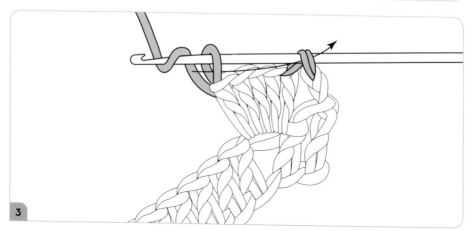

WORKING THE POPCORN STITCH

1 Make 5 dc into 1 st.

2 Remove hook from loop and insert into top of first dc.

3 Insert hook back into loop. Yarn over and pull through loop and first dc to form popcorn.

▶ **SEE ALSO**

Double crochet: page 76

Cables

Crochet cables are formed by working around the post stitches out of order, forming the distinctive twist. They can be used to adorn wraps/shawls, garments, cushion covers, blankets, and other home goods.

TIP

Be sure to work the stitches in the correct order in row 4, the row after the cable (twist) is made. They should be worked in the post-twist order.

To make crochet cables, work any multiple of six + five, for example 11, 17, or 23. Dc in 4th ch from hook and in each ch to end. Turn.

Row 1: Ch 3, dc in next st. * (Work front post dc (FPDC) around post of dc in row below) 4 times, dc in next 2 sts; rep from * to end.

Row 2: Ch 3, dc in next st. * (Work back post dc (BPDC) around post of dc in row below) 4 times, dc in next 2 sts; rep from * to end.

Row 3: Ch 3, dc in next st. * Work FPDC around post of 3rd st and 4th st from hook in row below, then work FPDC around post of 1st and 2nd st from hook in row below, dc in next 2 sts; rep from * to end.

Row 4: Repeat row 2. Repeat rows 1–4 to form the pattern.

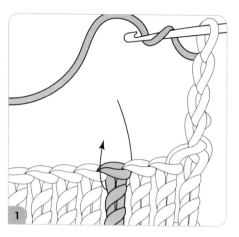

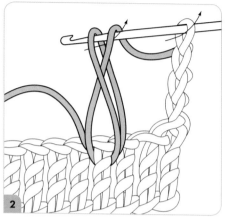

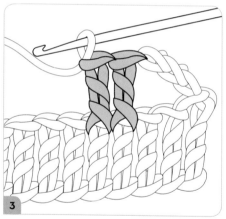

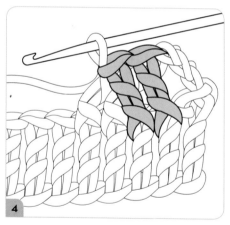

WORKING THE CABLE

1 Identify the 3rd dc in the row.

2 FPDC around 3rd dc.

3 FPDC around 4th dc.

4 FPDC around 1st dc, then second dc. Cable twist is now complete.

▶ **SEE ALSO**

Around the post: page 90

Gallery

Opposite:
Circular crochet rug
by Ana Gonçalves.

This page:
Left: Crochet hoop earrings
by Sita Brooks.

Below: Crochet pendant
light by Wendy Viel.

GALLERY

This page:
Left: Crochet detail necklace
by Nuta Orlova.

Below: Bead and crochet
necklace by Sandra
Vanden Broucke.

Opposite:
Crocheted pillow
by Wendy Viel.

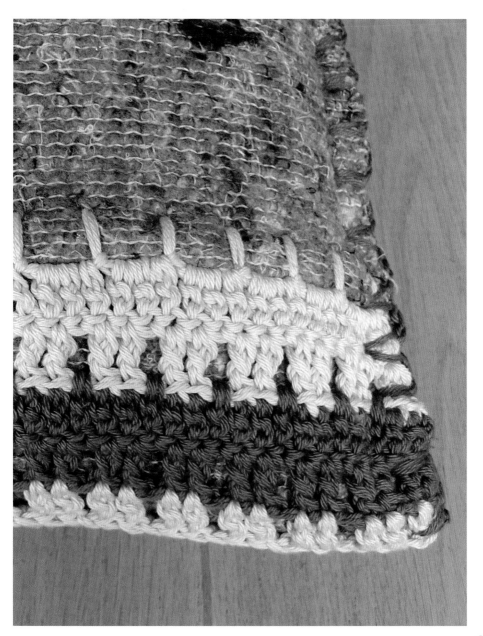

CHAPTER 9
Basic Shapes

Crochet lends itself well to making flat and 3-D shapes like squares, circles, hexagons, spheres, tubes, and more. Most of these shapes start at the center or top and work outward, increasing or decreasing at strategic points to achieve the shape desired. Use the flat motifs as building blocks to make bags, blankets, and even garments. 3-D shapes can be used to make toys, accessories, and embellishments.

Increasing and decreasing

"Increasing" and "decreasing" in crochet are used to make shapes other than flat, square, or rectangular fabric. You can use shaping to make garments and accessories, or to create circular crochet, tubular crochet, spherical crochet, hexagons, triangles, and many other shapes.

INCREASING

Increasing in crochet is easy. You simply work two or more stitches into the same stitch from the previous row/round. A single increase means working two stitches into one (increasing by one). A double increase means working three stitches into one (increasing by two), and so on.

DECREASING IN SINGLE CROCHET

To decrease in single crochet (sc2tog):

1 Insert the hook into the first stitch, YO, pull through a loop.

2 Insert the hook into the next stitch, YO, pull through a loop.

3 YO and pull through all three loops on hook. One stitch has now been decreased.

DECREASING IN DOUBLE CROCHET

To decrease in double crochet (dc2tog):

1 YO and insert the hook into the first stitch. YO and draw through a loop (3 loops on hook). YO and draw through two loops, leaving 2 on the hook.

2 YO and insert the hook into the next stitch. YO and draw through a loop (4 loops on

the hook). YO and draw through 2 loops, leaving 3 on the hook.

3 YO and pull through all three loops on hook. One stitch has been decreased.

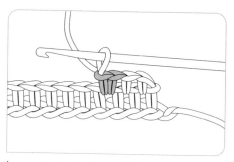

Increasing in single crochet

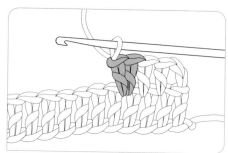

Increasing in double crochet

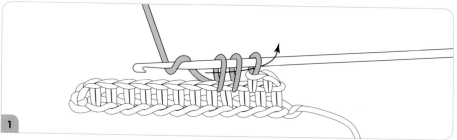

Decreasing in single crochet

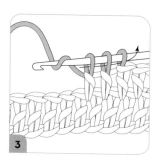

Decreasing in double crochet

▶ **SEE ALSO**

Single crochet: page 72
Double crochet: page 76

Flat shapes

Flat shapes such as squares and hexagons are often used to make blankets, but use your imagination and they can be incorporated into many diverse projects; why not create a cardigan from granny squares or crochet bunting with triangles?

FLAT CIRCLE

1   Ch 4, ss in first ch to form loop.

2   Ch 3, work 11 dc into loop (12 sts).

3   Ch 3, work 1 dc in same st as joining. 2 dc in each dc around (24 sts).

4   Ch 3, work 2 dc in next dc. * 1 dc in next dc, 2 dc in next dc; rep from * to end (36 sts).

5   Ch 3, work 1 dc in next dc, 2 dc in next dc. * 1 dc in each of next 2 dc, 2 dc in next dc; rep from * to end (48 sts).

6   Ch 3, work 1 dc in each of next 2 dc, 2 dc in next dc. * 1 dc in each of next 3 dc, 2 dc in next dc; rep from * to end (60 sts).

Fasten off, or continue in this manner, always working one additional single stitch between each increase per round, until the desired circumference is reached.

GRANNY SQUARE

1 Ch 4, ss in 1st ch to form loop.

2 Ch 3, 2 dc in loop. * Ch 2, 3 dc in loop; rep from * twice more, ch 2, ss in top of first ch-3 to join. Fasten off.

3 Join new color in any ch-2 corner space. Ch 3, work (2 dc, ch 2, 3 dc) in same sp as joining. * Ch 1, work (3 dc, ch 2, 3 dc) in next corner sp; rep from * twice more, ch 1, ss in top of first ch-3 to join. Fasten off.

4 Join new color in any ch-2 corner space. Ch 3, work (2 dc, ch 2, 3 dc) in same sp as joining. * Ch 1, 3 dc in next sp, ch 1, work (3 dc, ch 2, 3 dc) in next corner sp; rep from * twice more, ch 1, 3 dc in next sp, ch 1, ss in top of first ch-3 to join. Fasten off.

5 Join new color in any ch-2 corner space. Ch 3, work (2 dc, ch 2, 3 dc) in same sp as joining. * (Ch 1, 3 dc in next sp) twice, ch 1, work (3 dc, ch 2, 3 dc) in next corner sp; rep from * twice more, (ch 1, 3 dc in next sp) twice, ch 1, ss in top of first ch-3 to join. Fasten off.

6 Join new color in any ch-2 corner space. Ch 3, work (2 dc, ch 2, 3 dc) in same sp as joining. * (Ch 1, 3 dc in next sp) 3x, ch 1, ch 1, work (3 dc, ch 2, 3 dc) in next corner sp; rep from * twice more, (ch 1, 3 dc in next sp) 3x, ch 1, ss in top of first ch-3 to join. Fasten off.

Continue in this manner, always working (3 dc, ch 2, 3 dc) in corner spaces, 3 dc in side spaces, and ch 1 to move from space to space, until you reach the desired size.

FLAT SHAPES

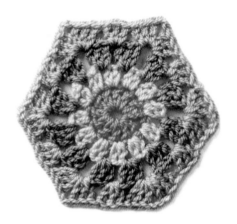

HEXAGON

1 Ch 4, ss in 1st ch to form loop.

2 Ch 3, work 11 dc in loop. Ss in top of first ch-3 to join. Fasten off.

3 Join new color in any st. Ch 3, 1 dc in same st as joining. * Ch 1, 2 dc in next st; rep from * to end. Fasten off.

4 Join new color in any ch-1 sp. Ch 3, work 2 dc in same sp as joining. * Ch 1, 3 dc in next ch-1 sp; rep from * to end. Fasten off.

5 Join new color in any ch-1 sp. Ch 3, work (2 dc, ch 2, 2 dc) in same sp as joining. * 3 dc in next space, (3 dc, ch 2, 3 dc) in next sp; rep from * 4 times more, 3 dc in next sp, ss in top of first ch-3 to join. Fasten off.

FLOWER

1 Ch 5, ss in 1st ch to form loop.

2 Ch 1, work 15 sc in loop. Ss in first sc to join.

3 * Ch 4, skip 2 sc, sc in next sc; rep from * to end (5 petal spaces). Fasten off.

4 Attach new yarn in any 4-ch petal space. * Work (1 sc, 1 hdc, 4 dc, 1 hdc, 1 sc) in petal space, ss in sc between petals; rep from * to end of round. Fasten off.

GRANNY TRIANGLE

1   Ch 4, ss in 1st ch to form loop.

2   Ch 3, 2 dc in loop. * Ch 3, 3 dc in loop;
    rep from * once more, ch 3, ss in top of
    first ch-3 to join.

3   Ss in next 2 sts and into next ch-3 sp.
    Ch 3, work (2 dc, ch 3, 3 dc) in same sp.
    * Ch 3, work (3 dc, ch 3, 3 dc) in next sp;
    rep from * once more, ch 3, ss in top of
    first ch-3 to join.

4   Ss in next 2 sts and into next ch-3 sp.
    Ch 3, work (2 dc, ch 3, 3 dc) in same sp.
    * Ch 2, 3 dc in next sp, ch 2, work (3 dc,
    ch 3, 3 dc) in next sp; rep from * once
    more, ch 2, 3 dc in next sp, ch 2, ss in top
    of first ch-3 to join.

5   Ss in next 2 sts and into next ch-3 sp.
    Ch 3, work (2 dc, ch 3, 3 dc) in same sp.
    * (Ch 2, 3 dc in next sp) twice, ch 2, work
    (3 dc, ch 3, 3 dc) in next sp; rep from *
    once more, (ch 2, 3 dc in next sp) twice,
    ch 2, ss in top of first ch-3 to join.
    Fasten off.

SEMICIRCLE

1   Ch 3, ss in 1st ch to form loop.

2   Ch 3, work 5 dc in loop, turn (6 sts).

3   Ch 3, dc in same st. 2 dc in each st to end,
    turn (12 sts).

4   Ch 3, 2 dc in next st, * 1 dc in next st,
    2 dc in next st; rep from * to end, turn
    (18 sts).

5   Ch 3, dc in next st, 2 dc in next st. * 1 dc
    in each of next 2 sts, 2 dc in next st; rep
    from * to end, turn (24 sts).

6   Ch 3, 1 dc in each of next 2 sts, 2 dc in
    next st. * 1 dc in each of next 3 sts, 2 dc
    in next st; rep from * to end, turn (30 sts).
    Fasten off.

FLAT SHAPES

CLOSED SQUARE

1 Ch 4, ss in 1st ch to form loop.

2 Ch 3, 2 dc in loop. * Ch 2, 3 dc in loop; rep from * twice more, ch 2, ss in top of first ch-3 to join.

3 Ch 3, * dc in each st to next corner sp. Work (2 dc, ch 2, 2 dc) in corner sp; rep from * 3x more, dc in each st to end, ss in top of first ch-3 to join.

Rep last round until the desired size is reached. The sample worked four total rounds.

OVAL

Note: Use a stitch marker throughout to mark the first stitch of each round.

1 Ch 4, sk 1 ch, sc in each of next 3 chs, 3 sc in next ch. Working down other side of ch, sc in each of next 3 chs, 3 sc in last ch (12 sts).

2 (Sc in each of next 3 sts, 2 sc in each of next 3 sts) twice (18 sts).

3 (Sc in each of next 3 sts, [1 sc in next st, 2 sc in next st] 3x) twice (24 sts).

4 (Sc in each of next 3 sts, [1 sc in each of next 2 sts, 2 sc in next st] 3x) twice (30 sts).

5 (Sc in each of next 3 sts, [1 sc in each of next 3 sts, 2 sc in next st] 3x) twice (36 sts).

Fasten off, or continue in this manner until the desired size is reached.

FLOWERY SQUARE

1 Ch 4, ss in 1st ch to form loop.

2 Ch 1, 8 sc in loop. Ss in 1st sc to join.

3 * Ch 4, sk 1 st, ss in next st; rep from * to end (4 petal spaces).

4 * Work (1 sc, 1 hdc, 2 dc, 1 hdc, 1 sc) in next petal sp; rep from * to end. Ss in 1st sc to join.

5 Ss into back of same st. * Ch 3. Working behind petal, ss between petals; rep from * to end (4 petal spaces).

6 * Work (1 sc, 1 hdc, 4 dc, 1 hdc, 1 sc) in next petal space; rep from * to end. Ss in 1st sc to join.

7 Ss into back of same st. * Ch 4. Working behind petal, ss between petals; rep from * to end (4 petal spaces).

8 * Work (1 sc, 1 hdc, 6 dc, 1 hdc, 1 sc) in next petal space; rep from * to end. Ss in 1st sc to join.

9 Rep round 7.

10 Ss into next ch sp. Ch 3, work (2 dc, ch 2, 3 dc) in same sp. * Work (3 dc, ch 2, 3 dc) in next sp; rep from * twice more. Ss in top of first ch-3 to join.

11 Ch 3, * dc in each st to next corner sp. Work (2 dc, ch 2, 2 dc) in corner sp; rep from * 3x more, dc in each st to end, ss in top of first ch-3 to join.

Rep last round once more (as in sample) or to desired size. Fasten off.

FLAT SHAPES

SMALL HEART

Note: Begin this pattern with a long tail. Weave the beginning of tail through the stitches in the center and pull tight to close the center hole when the heart is finished.

1   Leaving a long tail, ch 3, ss in 1st ch to form loop.

2   Ch 1, work (3 dc, 4 sc, 1 dc, 4 sc, 3 dc) in loop. Ch 1, ss in loop.

3   Sc in next st, hdc in next st, (hdc, dc) in next st, (dc, hdc) in next st, hdc in next 4 sts, (hdc, dc, hdc) in next st, hdc in next 4 sts, (hdc, dc) in next st, (dc, hdc) in next st, hdc in next st, sc in next st. Ss in 1st ss to join. Fasten off.

TIP

When working flat shapes in the round, try to picture the steps of each round visually as well as using the text. You are often working a certain set of instructions, then repeating those instructions around the piece, so it may be easier to use the piece in your hands as a visual guide than to be continually scanning the text.

Three-dimensional shapes

Three-dimensional shapes are perfect for toys: you can create a huge variety of animals, birds, and other items with the simplest spheres and tubes. But the same techniques used here can also be used to make hats, socks, and other accessories.

SPHERE

Note: use a stitch marker throughout to mark first stitch of round.

1 Ch 2, work 6 sc into 2nd ch from hook.

2 2 sc in each sc around (12 sts).

3 * 1 sc in next sc, 2 sc in next sc; rep from * to end (18 sts).

4 * 1 sc in each of next 2 sc, 2 sc in next sc; rep from * to end (24 sts).

5 * 1 sc in each of next 3 sc, 2 sc in next sc; rep from * to end (30 sts).

6-11 sc in each sc around (30 sts).

12 * 1 sc in each of next 3 sc, sc2tog; rep from * to end (24 sts).

13 * 1 sc in each of next 2 sc, sc2tog; rep from * to end (18 sts).

14 * 1 sc in next sc, sc2tog; rep from * to end (12 sts). Stuff firmly with toy stuffing.

15 Sc2tog around (6 sts). Cut the yarn, leaving a long tail. Use the tail to close the last 6 sts, and lose the inside sphere.

THREE-DIMENSIONAL SHAPES

HOURGLASS SHAPE

Note: Use a stitch marker throughout to mark first stitch of each round.

1 Ch 2, work 6 sc into 2nd ch from hook.

2 2 sc in each sc around (12 sts).

3 * 1 sc in next sc, 2 sc in next sc; rep from * to end (18 sts).

4 * 1 sc in each of next 2 sc, 2 sc in next sc; rep from * to end (24 sts).

5 * 1 sc in each of next 3 sc, 2 sc in next sc; rep from * to end (30 sts).

6-10 1 sc in each sc around (30 sts).

11 * 1 sc in each of next 3 sc, sc2tog; rep from * to end (24 sts).

12 * 1 sc in each of next 2 sc, sc2tog; rep from * to end (18 sts).

13-15 1 sc in each sc around (18 sts).

16 * 1 sc in each of next 2 sc, 2 sc in next sc; rep from * to end (24 sts).

17 * 1 sc in each of next 3 sc, 2 sc in next sc; rep from * to end (30 sts).

18-22 1 sc in each sc around (30 sts).

23 * 1 sc in each of next 3 sc, sc2tog; rep from * to end (24 sts).

24 * 1 sc in each of next 2 sc, sc2tog; rep from * to end (18 sts).

25 * 1 sc in next sc, sc2tog; rep from * to end (12 sts).

Stuff firmly with toy stuffing.

26 sc2tog around (6 sts).

Cut the yarn, leaving a long tail. Use the tail to close the last 6 sts and lose the inside hourglass.

TUBE

Note: use a stitch marker throughout to mark the first stitch of each round.

1 Ch 2, work 6 sc into 2nd ch from hook.

2 2 sc in each sc around (12 sts).

3 * 1 sc in next st, 2 sc in next st; rep from * to end (18 sts).

4-18 sc in each sc around (18 sts).

(The above even rounds can be repeated until desired length is reached. If making a very long tube, stuff at intervals.)

19 * 1 sc in next sc, sc2tog; rep from * to end (12 sts).

Stuff firmly with toy stuffing.

20 Sc2tog around (6 sts).

Cut the yarn, leaving a long tail. Use the tail to close the last 6 sts, and close inside the sphere.

TIP

It is vital to use a stitch marker when working 3-D shapes, as they are often made in single crochet, and it is difficult to see the beginning of the round without a marker. When marking the first stitch of a round, insert the marker under the legs of the "v" just behind the loop on the hook.

CHAPTER 10
Borders and Edges

Crochet lends itself well to borders and edgings, particularly on items such as garments or blankets where the finished edge will be on display. These can be easily added to pieces you have crocheted or knitted yourself, or to commercially made garments, accessories, and home goods.

Borders

Borders and edgings are very easy to create with crochet, and they can be added to knitted and woven goods as well as crocheted items. You can also add a simple embroidered edge (like blanket stitch) to a commercially woven piece, like a pillowcase, and then use the embroidered stitches as a base for crochet done with thin cotton to make a lacy edging.

▶ **SEE ALSO**
Single crochet: page 72
Single crochet rows: page 114
Picot: page 146

SINGLE CROCHET

This can be worked over any number of stitches. It makes a clean, tailored edge.

With a contrasting color, attach the yarn and insert the hook into the first stitch of the edge to be worked.

Ch 1, and work single crochet evenly across the edge. Fasten off.

SHELL

This can be worked over any multiple of three stitches. Shell edging will add a soft, rounded, feminine touch to a project.

With a contrasting color, attach the yarn and insert the hook into the first stitch of the edge to be worked.

Ch 1, sc in same st. * Skip 2 sts, 5 dc in next st. Skip 2 sts, 1 sc in next st. Rep from * to end of edge. Fasten off.

SHELL WITH PICOT

This can be worked over any multiple of three stitches. Adding the picot to a traditional shell edging gives an extra decorative detail.

With a contrasting color, attach the yarn and insert the hook into the first stitch of the edge to be worked.

Ch 1, sc in same st. * Skip 2 sts, work (3dc, ch 4, ss in 1st ch, 2 dc) in next st, skip 2 sts, 1 sc in next st. Rep from * to end of edge. Fasten off.

BORDERS

CRAB STITCH

This can be worked over any number of stitches. Crab stitch makes an attractive edging on blankets.

With a contrasting color, attach the yarn and insert the hook into the **last** stitch of the edge to be worked. Ch 1, sc in same st. Working left to right if you are right-handed and right to left if you are left-handed, then sc in each st across edge. Fasten off.

PICOT

This can be worked over any number of stitches. A picot edge makes a crocheted item look elegantly finished.

With a contrasting color, attach the yarn and insert the hook into the first stitch of the edge to be worked. Ch 1, sc in same st. Ch 3, ss in 1st ch (picot made). * Sc in next st, ch 3, ss in 1st ch; rep from * to end of edge. Fasten off.

▶ **SEE ALSO**
Shell with picot: page 145

BOBBLE

This can be worked over any even number of stitches. Bobble edging looks very sweet on baby garments.

Dc3tog: YO, insert in st to be worked. YO, pull up a loop, YO, pull through 2 loops, (YO, insert into same st, YO, pull up a loop, YO, pull through 2 loops) twice, YO, pull through all 4 loops on hook.

Dc4tog: YO, insert in st to be worked. YO, pull up a loop, YO, pull through 2 loops, (YO, insert into same st, YO, pull up a loop, YO, pull through 2 loops) 3x, YO, pull through all 4 loops on hook.

With a contrasting color, attach the yarn and insert the hook into the first stitch of edge to be worked. Ch 3, dc3tog in same st. * Ch 1, skip 1 st, dc4tog in next st; rep from * to end of edge. Fasten off.

TROUBLESHOOTING

"How can I choose a trim without counting stitches?" Some edgings can only be worked over a certain number or multiple of stitches. Be sure that your edging will work on the number of stitches in the item to be edged. You can adjust slightly by one or two stitches, but be sure the number in question is close to the number needed for that edging.

Corners

To turn a corner in crochet, you need to add stitches, chains, or a combination of the two to allow the corner to lie flat and retain its point.

When working an edging on a flat square of crochet worked in rows, try this method:

1 Attach new yarn and work the stitch desired (in the sample shown here, the edging was worked in single crochet) to last stitch of side.

2 In the last stitch, work 2 sc, ch 1, 2 sc.

3 Working down next side, sc in each st to end.

4 Repeat for all sides to be edged.

TROUBLESHOOTING

"The corners of my crochet piece are messy and not sharp." Remember that you need to increase around a corner with stitches, chains, or a combination of both to allow the corner to retain its point. If you are working an edging of single crochet, for example, and you simply work one single crochet into each stitch around the corner, the corner will become rounded. Try using this corner tutorial instead.

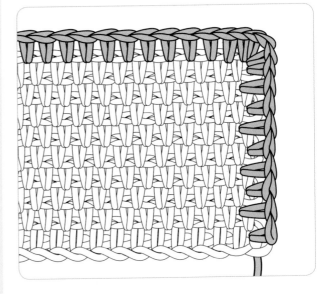

▶ **SEE ALSO**
Closed square: page 136

Buttonholes

To make a buttonhole in crochet, you will skip the number of stitches equivalent to just smaller than the button to be used, then chain the same number of stitches skipped, then continue the row/round. On the following row/round, work into the chains as you would stitches.

Try this method (worked in single crochet):

1　Sc across row to desired placement for buttonhole.

2　Ch 2, sk 2 sts.

3　Continue in sc across row.

4　On the following row, sc in each st to chs, sc in each ch, sc to end of row. The buttonhole is now complete.

TROUBLESHOOTING

"My buttonholes are too big!" Many crocheters make the mistake of making their buttonhole the same size as the button to be used. Actually, a buttonhole should be slightly smaller than the button, so it has to stretch to allow the button to pass through. Otherwise, the button will slip through too easily and the piece will not stay buttoned.

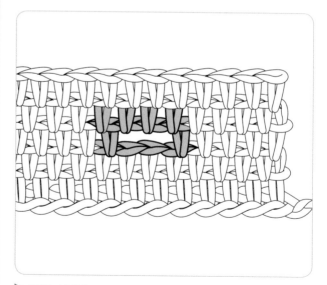

▶ **SEE ALSO**
Buttons: page 49
Adding buttons: page 158

Pockets

There are two different ways to make pockets on a crocheted piece—a patch pocket or an internal pocket.

TO MAKE A PATCH POCKET

1 Make a square of crochet in your choice of stitch, to the size of the pocket desired.

2 Use small, neat whip stitches to attach the pocket to the crocheted piece.

3 Alternatively, use a decorative stitch like blanket stitch in the same or contrasting color to attach the pocket.

TIP

Using single crochet will make the pocket more dense and secure, which will be better for holding smaller items.

Remember that attaching a patch pocket is one of the few instances where your stitching/seaming will show on the outside of the piece. It is important to take your time and experiment with different attaching stitches until you find the one that works best for that piece.

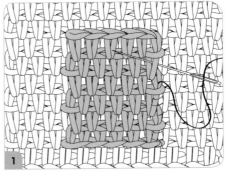

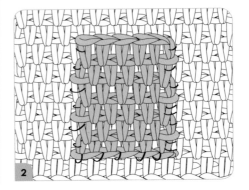

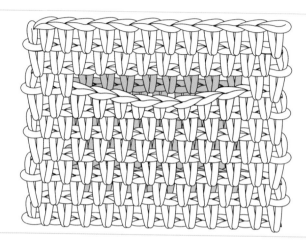

TO MAKE AN INTERNAL POCKET

1 When working the main body of the garment, work two rows as follows:

a. Work in your choice of stitch to the area where you want the pocket to be placed. Skip the number of stitches equivalent to the width of the pocket desired, and chain the number of stitches skipped. Continue working across the row.

b. In the next row, work stitches into the chains as you would into stitches.

2 After the main body is finished, pick up stitches to make the pocket lining as follows:

a. Turn piece so WS is facing you. Insert hook into front loop only of first st skipped, and, using same or contrasting color (this sample uses a contrasting color), work sc in front loop of each st skipped, 2 sc into side between skipped stitches and chains, sc in unused side of each ch made in section a of part 1, and 2 sc in other side between chains and skipped stitches.

b. Join to work in the round by beginning the next round in the first stitch made in section a of part 2. Work one sc in each sc around, working even rounds until pocket is desired depth, ending at side edge of pocket.

c. Inserting hook through both layers of pocket, ss across each st to end. Fasten off and weave in ends.

▶ **SEE ALSO**
Joining methods: page 176

CHAPTER 11
Adding Trims and Embellishments

Once a piece is finished, you can add trims and embellishments to enhance the final product. You can either make these yourself, or purchase them pre made. Remember that the laundering requirements for embellished garments and accessories may change after the trims are added. It is also important to note that embellishments and trims that can be removed and swallowed should not be added to items for babies or small children.

Adding beads and sequins

Using beads and sequins are a lovely way to add sparkle and visual interest to crocheted fabric. Beads can be added while crocheting, or sewn on after the fact.

BEADS

To add beads while crocheting, string the beads onto the yarn before beginning. (**Note:** when purchasing beads to be used in this way, ensure the beads have a large enough hole to allow the yarn and the needle used to string them to pass through.)

Then try this method (using single crochet):

1   Insert into next st, YO, and draw through a loop.

2   Bring bead up to sit against back of work.

3   YO and pull through both loops, securing the bead. The bead will rest at the back of the fabric, so you need to place the beads where you'd like them to go while working the opposite side of the rows/rounds.

To add beads after the piece has been finished, use sewing thread that matches your yarn. Attach the beads securely, working the thread through the yarn in between the beads so it does not show.

2

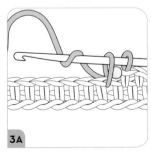

3A

3B

SEQUINS

Most sequins do not have a big enough hole to allow them to be threaded onto yarn (unless you are using a very thin crochet cotton), so you will need to sew them on after the fact. Sew sequins to your fabric using sewing thread that matches your yarn. Attach them securely, working the thread through the yarn in between the sequins so it does not show.

TIP

Remember that adding embellishments like beads and sequins to crocheted fabric will change how you launder a garment. Consider whether it is practical to have to hand-wash a child's garment, for example. Also consider the stitch pattern: a very busy stitch pattern will not show these embellishments to their best. Finally, ensure that all items are attached securely to the fabric, particularly if they are to be given to a baby.

 SEE ALSO
Sequins and beads: page 50

Adding pompoms

Pompoms can be purchased pre made or you can easily make them yourself.

TO MAKE A POMPOM

1 Cut out two donut-shaped pieces of sturdy cardboard.

2 Using the yarn desired for your pompom, wind it around both cardboard rings firmly until it is almost covered.

3 Using a pair of sharp scissors, cut the yarn between the two layers of cardboard. Do not pull the layers apart.

4 Pass a length of yarn or matching sewing thread between the two layers of cardboard. Tie tightly.

5 Cut a slit in each of the cardboard pieces that runs from the edge to the center hole. Pull off the cardboard pieces and fluff out the pompom.

There are commercially available pompom makers that use the same method as above, making the process easier.

TO ATTACH THE POMPOMS TO YOUR CROCHETED PIECE

If you made your own pompoms, leave a long tail of yarn and use this tail to attach the pompom to the piece securely.

If you did not make your pompom, use a matching length of yarn and needle. Push the needle through the middle of the pompom several times, threading it onto the yarn, and use the yarn to secure the pompom to the piece.

▶ **SEE ALSO**
Pompoms: page 51

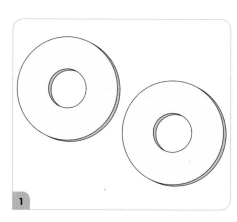

1

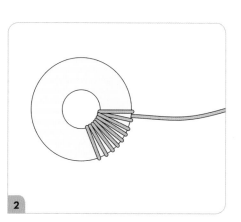

2

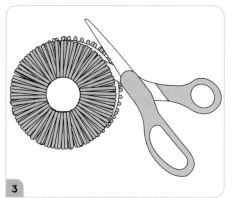

3

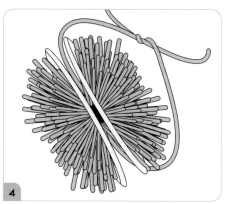

4

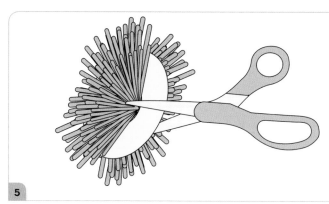

5

Adding buttons

Buttons can be used functionally, to open and close an item, or decoratively as you would use beads or sequins.

When placing buttons that are to be matched up with corresponding buttonholes, mark the place for the button with a pin before sewing on.

TO SECURE A BUTTON TO A PIECE OF CROCHETED FABRIC

1   Use a length of sewing thread to match the button (most yarn needles will not pass through the holes in a button).

2   Whether using a flat or shank button, be sure to pass the thread through it several times and secure it at the back of the piece so it will not come off while laundering the item.

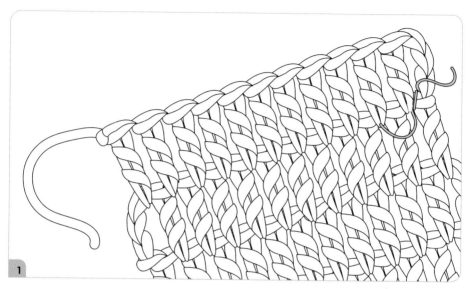

1

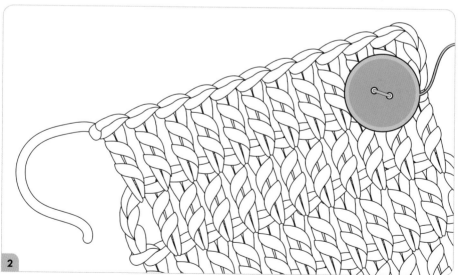

2

▶ **SEE ALSO**

Buttons: page 49
Buttonholes: page 149

Adding cords

Cords can be used in many applications in crochet: as drawstrings in hooded garments, across a bodice to add shaping, or to close a drawstring bag.

Cords for drawstrings and edgings can be purchased pre made or you can make them yourself.

TO MAKE A CORD

1 Chain the length desired for the cord.

2 For a thin cord, sk first ch and work ss into each ch to end. For a thicker cord, sk first ch and work sc into each ch to end.

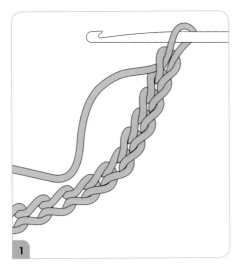

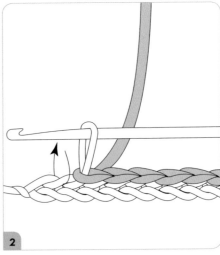

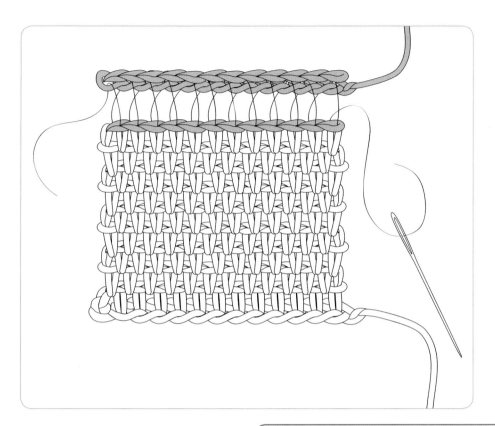

TO ATTACH A PRE MADE OR HANDMADE CORD TO A PIECE OF CROCHET

Using whip stitch and a length of sewing thread to match the yarn, go through the underside of the cord and then through the top of the side to be edged. Repeat across length to be edged.

TIP

To make a cord for a drawstring, be sure to make the cord at least 12 in/30 cm longer than length of the crocheted piece.

▶ SEE ALSO

Cords: page 51

Adding fringe

Adding fringe is a quick and easy way to add visual appeal to a piece of crochet. Even a beginner crocheter can make fringe with ease!

MAKING YOUR OWN FRINGE

Fringe can be purchased pre made or you can make it yourself using this method.

1   Cut lengths of yarn double the length of the fringe desired. Cut one or two lengths for each stitch to be fringed.

2   Insert the hook into the first stitch to be fringed. YO with one or two lengths of fringe, holding all ends in the yarn-holding hand.

3   Pull the fringe through a loop. Do not pull through any of the pieces entirely.

4   YO with all ends of the fringe and pull through the loop. Tighten firmly.

5   After adding all the fringe, trim evenly.

TO ATTACH PRE MADE FRINGE

Using whip or blanket stitch and a length of sewing thread to match the yarn, attach securely to wrong side of edge to be fringed.

MAKING YOUR OWN FRINGE

1

2

3

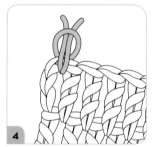

4

5

TO ATTACH PRE MADE FRINGE

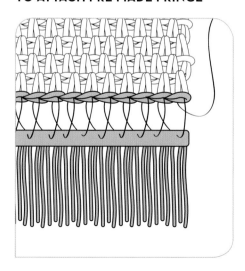

▶ **SEE ALSO**

Fringes and tassels: page 50

Adding zippers

Zippers can be attached by hand or by using a sewing machine. If you are using a sewing machine, be sure to use a zipper foot that will accommodate thicker crocheted fabric.

TO ATTACH A ZIPPER WITH A MACHINE

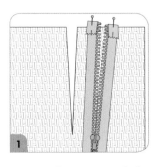
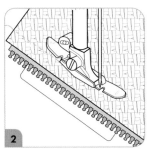

1 Open the zipper. With the zipper pull facing up and the WS of the crochet facing, insert one side of the zipper's fabric edge underneath the crocheted edge and pin it in place.

2 Using a zipper foot and matching thread, sew the zipper into place as close to the edge as possible. Ensure that the zip teeth barely show from the RS of the fabric.

3 Tuck under any ends that are too long and sew them into place.

TO ATTACH A ZIPPER BY HAND

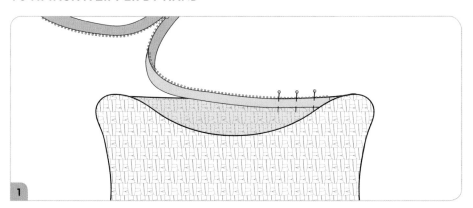

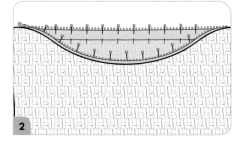

1 Open the zipper. With the zipper pull facing up, insert one side of the zipper's fabric edge underneath the crocheted edge and pin it in place.

2 Using a length of sewing thread and small, neat whip stitches, sew the edge of the crochet to the vertical center of the zipper's fabric edge.

3 Work down the other side of the zipper in the same way.

4 Pay special attention to the non-pull end of the zipper, sewing the short edge securely.

5 If attaching a zipper that will need to open completely (as in the front of a cardigan), sew both sides separately, then trim the short end of the zipper so it does not show under the crochet fabric.

▶ **SEE ALSO**

Zippers: page 50

Adding tassels

Tassels for embellishment can be purchased pre made or you can make them yourself.

TO MAKE A TASSEL

1 Cut lengths of yarn double the length of the tassel desired.

2 Fold the lengths in half and use another length to tie the lengths together.

3 Use another length to tie the bundle of yarn several times, until it is as tight as desired. You can also use a dab of fabric glue to keep the length used to tie the bundle secure.

4 Trim the edges evenly.

TIP

Pre made tassels are an easy alternative to making your own. To attach these to a crochet piece, all you need to do is sew them securely to your crochet using a length of yarn or sewing thread in a matching color.

1

2

3

4

▶ **SEE ALSO**

Fringes and tassels: page 50

CHAPTER 12
Finishing

Finishing crocheted items cleanly and attractively is just as important as the construction of the individual elements in terms of the final look. Work carefully when you are finishing your piece to ensure it looks as professional as possible.

Fastening off and weaving ends

All crochet projects require you to fasten off the yarn and weave in your ends. With practice, this can be achieved neatly and efficiently. Be sure to weave in the tail securely, ensuring it will not come loose with laundering or during use.

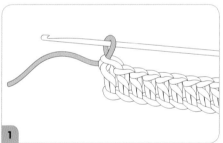

1

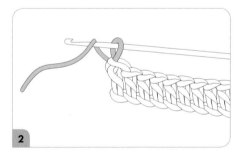

2

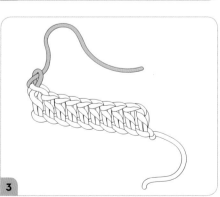

3

FASTENING OFF

1 Cut the yarn, leaving a minimum 4 in/ 10 cm tail.

2 YO and draw the tail all the way through the loop on the hook, securing the last loop.

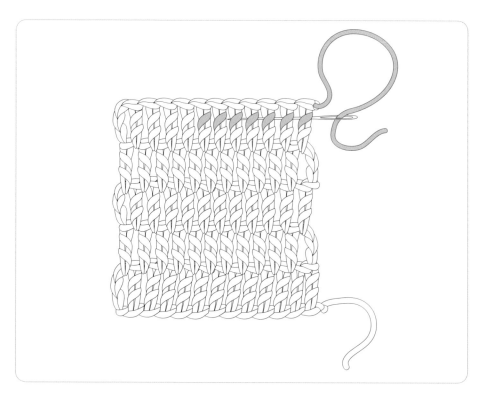

WEAVE IN ENDS

1 Thread the tail onto the yarn needle.

2 Weave in a minimum of 2 in/5 cm or 10 sts.

3 Cut the yarn close to the work, being careful not to cut
   the main fabric.

▶ **SEE ALSO**

Leaving a tail: page 62

Care and maintenance: page 178

Blocking

Blocking is a process that can transform your crochet. When done properly, it will correct problems with tension, allow edges to sit straight and true, and open up openwork stitch patterns. Blocking works best when used on natural-fiber yarns. If you are happy with the appearance of the fabric when finished, it is not necessary to block, but it is often beneficial to the final look of the piece. You can block separate pieces before seaming them together; the blocking will likely help to make the edges easier to seam.

Blocking works because natural fiber yarns have memory, which means they will lock into place when pinned into shape while wet and (optionally) steamed, then allowed to dry. After washing, the piece will need to be reblocked, although some memory from the original blocking can sometimes remain.

1 Wash the piece by hand in cold water and detergent suitable for the fiber content of the yarn, or spray the piece with a water bottle until wet through. If you have washed it, roll the piece in a towel and press out excess water, taking care not to twist, wring, or pull the fabric.

2 Place the piece on a flat surface like an ironing board, towel, or mat, and then pin it out flat: use a schematic if available to ensure correct sizing. Use enough pins to hold the edges straight. Allow the fabric to lie flat without excessive stretching (unless the piece has a stitch pattern that benefits from this, like a lace or openwork item).

3 If the yarn used has more than 40% synthetic content, allow the fabric to dry completely before removing the pins. **It is vital not to iron synthetic yarn, as it will be ruined.** If the yarn used has more than 60% natural fiber, you can use a steam iron to steam the piece before allowing it to dry. Glide the iron over the surface of the fabric without pressing down—you can use a pressing cloth to protect particularly hairy/fuzzy fabric.

1

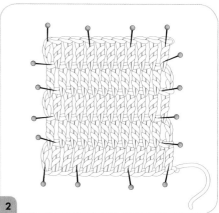

2

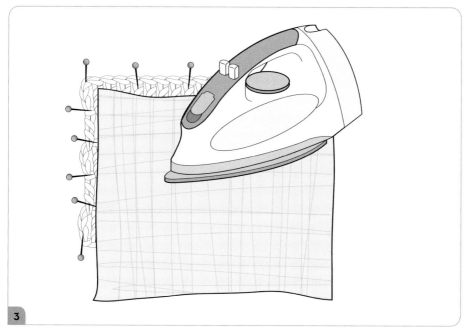

3

▶ **SEE ALSO**
Fiber content: page 28

Joining methods

Joining is a skill that will improve with practice. Joining well will make a huge difference in the final look of your crocheted piece. It is worth learning several methods for joining, and using the appropriate method in each circumstance. You can use a crochet hook, or a yarn needle and length of yarn to join.

CROCHETED JOINS

Crocheted joins are strong and look neat, although they are generally visible. They are also faster and more efficient than sewn joins. It is important not to make crocheted joins too tight, as the work will pull in at the edges of the seam and not lie flat. Crocheted joins can be worked on the RS or WS of the fabric; experiment with both to see which you prefer.

SLIP STITCH JOIN

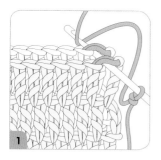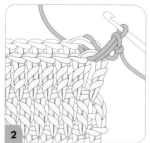

SINGLE CROCHET JOIN

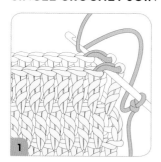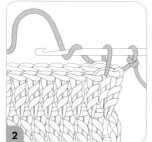

SLIP STITCH JOIN

The seam created by a slip stitch join will lie flat, but will lean to one side of the join rather than sitting between the two pieces joined.

1 Insert the crochet hook through both equivalent stitches of pieces to be joined. YO and pull through both stitches and the loop on the hook.

2 Continue in this manner, inserting into each sequential stitch across sides to be joined.

SINGLE CROCHET JOIN

The seam created by a single crochet join sits up from the surface of the fabric, but will lie centered between the two pieces joined.

1 Insert the crochet hook through both equivalent stitches of pieces to be joined. YO and pull through both stitches.

2 YO again and pull through both remaining loops.

3 Continue in this manner, inserting into each sequential stitch across the sides to be joined.

SEWN JOINS

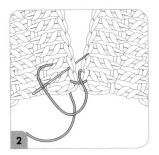

MATTRESS STITCH

Mattress stitch works well in most joining situations, particularly the side seams of a garment, hat, cowl, or cushion cover.

1   Work with RS facing throughout. Starting at the bottom of the seams to be worked and using a separate length of yarn, pull the yarn through, leaving a minimum of 4 in/10 cm tail.

2   Beginning on one side, working from bottom to top, insert under first stitch, then the equivalent stitch on the other piece.

3   Continue in this manner, lacing through equivalent stitches on either side in sequence and pulling tight at intervals. Weave in tails at both ends.

The seam will be created on the other side, which is why it is important to have RS facing.

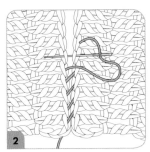

WHIP STITCH

Whip stitch can easily look untidy so avoid it unless there is no other choice, such as when attaching a patch pocket to a piece of crocheted fabric. It is important to make small, neat stitches that are evenly spaced.

1   Hold the pieces to be seamed together with WS facing. Using a separate length of yarn, pull yarn through, leaving a minimum of 4 in/10 cm tail.

2   Always inserting the needle from behind the two pieces, insert close to the edge and pull through both layers, looping the yarn around the edge. Angle the stitches so that they create diagonal lines.

3   Continue in this manner to the end of the seam, and then weave in the tails at both ends.

The seam will be created on the same side, so ensure wrong sides are facing.

BACKSTITCH

Backstitch is a good joining choice for seams that need to be particularly strong, such as bag bottoms or shoulder seams. It makes a thick seam so should not be used in situations where bulk is not desired.

1   Hold the pieces to be seamed together with WS facing. Using a separate length of yarn, pull yarn through, leaving a minimum of 4 in/10 cm tail.

2   Take a small stitch around the first stitch and through both layers, drawing the yarn through to the back.

3   Move ahead one stitch length along the seam and draw the yarn through to the front.

4   Insert the needle back at the end of the first stitch and draw the yarn through to the back.

5   Continue in this manner, always moving one stitch ahead when inserting through to the front, and closing the gap when inserting through to the back, to the end of the seam. Weave in the tails at both ends.

TIP

If the yarn you used to crochet the piece is not ideal for joining (too fuzzy/textured/unplied), you can use a matching length of sewing thread (preferably with some synthetic content for strength) instead.

Care and maintenance

Properly caring for a crocheted item depends on the yarn used, the embellishments added, and the finishing techniques incorporated.

YARN

Take note of the laundering information given on the ball band. It is a good idea to keep a notebook with all your handmade items listed and their laundering information (along with a length of the yarn used if possible).

You should wash animal fiber yarn with care, avoiding felting by not agitating the fabric too much. Hand washing is always safest, but the wool cycle on your washing machine can be used if the yarn is not too fuzzy/unplied.

EMBELLISHMENTS

It is advisable to hand launder any items that incorporate beads, sequins, ribbons, or buttons. You can make embellishments like tassels removable for washing.

FINISHING TECHNIQUES

If the item has been blocked previously, it will likely need reblocking after laundering.

MOTH CONTROL

Use an anti-moth product when storing animal fiber crochet. Check regularly for any infestation and for any tell-tale holes. If moths or holes are seen, freeze the item to kill the moth eggs before repairing.

TIP

When giving a crocheted item as a gift, provide the recipient with laundering information as well.

▶ **SEE ALSO**
Fiber content: page 28
Adding trims and embellishments: page 152

SECTION 3
RESOURCES

Online resources

WEBSITES

Crochet Guild of America
www.crochet.org

Ravelry
www.ravelry.com

Craft Yarn Council
www.craftyarncouncil.com

Yarn Standards
www.yarnstandards.com

Annie's Crafts
www.anniescatalog.com

Needlecraft University
www.needlecraftuniversity.com

Knitting and Crochet Guild
www.kcguild.org.uk

Clover USA
www.clover-usa.com

TRADE SHOWS

The Knit & Crochet Show
www.knitandcrochetshow.com

Craft and Hobby Association
www.craftandhobby.org

Craft and Quilt Fair
www.craftevents.com.au

Maker Faire
www.makerfaire.com

International Craft and Hobby Fair
www.ichf.co.uk

Craft Hobby + Stitch International
www.chsi.co.uk

Patterns and supplies

Michael's
www.michaels.com

Jo-Ann
www.joann.com

Hobby Lobby
www.hobbylobby.com

Knitting Warehouse
www.knitting-warehouse.com

Hobbycraft
www.hobbycraft.co.uk

Pack Lane Wool and Crafts
www.packlanewool.co.uk

The Crochet Chain
www.thecrochetchain.co.uk

Scarlet Dash
www.scarletdash.co.uk

Adriafil
www.adriafil.com

Bendigo Woolen Mills
www.bendigowoolenmills.com.au

Brown Sheep Company
www.brownsheep.com

Excelana
www.excelana.com

Holst Garn
www.holstgran.dk

Marion Foale Yarns
www.marionfoaleyarn.com

Quince & Co.
www.quinceandco.com

Sirdar
www.sirdar.co.uk

Virtual Yarns
www.virtualyarns.com

Simplicity
www.simplicity.com

Crochet Pattern Central
www.crochetpatterncentral.com

Lion Brand
www.lionbrand.com

Bernat
www.bernat.com

Rowan
www.knitrowan.com

Further reading

BOOKS

Brown, Nancy, *The Crocheter's Companion*, Interweave Press (2002)

Burger, Deborah, *Crochet 101*, Creative Publishing International (2012)

Chin, Lily, *Lily Chin's Crochet Tips & Tricks*, Potter Craft (2009)

Cosh, Sylvia and Walters, James, *The Crochet Workbook*, St. Martins Griffin (1990)

Eaton, Jan, *200 Crochet Tips, Techniques & Trade Secrets*, St. Martins Griffin (2007)

Eckman, Edie, *The Crochet Answer Book*, Storey Publishing (2005)

Hubert, Margaret, *The Complete Photo Guide to Crochet*, Creative Publishing International (2010)

Kelm, Cecily, *Teach Yourself Visually Crochet*, Visual (2011)

Kooler, Donna, *Encyclopedia of Crochet*, Leisure Arts (2002)

Turner, Pauline, *How to Crochet*, Collins & Brown (2001)

MAGAZINES

The Art of Crochet
www.theartofcrochet.com

Crochet Today
www.crochettoday.com

Crochet World
www.crochet-world.com

Duplet, Zhurnal
www.duplet-crochet.com

Inside Crochet
www.insidecrochet.co.uk

Interweave Crochet
www.crochetme.com

Mollie Makes
www.molliemakes.com

Rowan Knitting and Crochet Magazine
www.knitrowan.com/designs-and-patterns/magazines

Simply Crochet Magazine
www.simplycrochetmag.co.uk

Contributor index

Bernadette Ambergen
www.BernioliesDesigns.etsy.com

Sita Brooks
www.DivaishbySitaB.etsy.com

Ana Gonçalves
www.NavitrineShop.etsy.com

Ashley Jackson Rodriguez
www.12Charlotte.etsy.com

Şennur Öğüşlü
www.sostyle.etsy.com

Nuta Orlova
www.EjaEjovna.etsy.com

Sandra Vanden Broucke
www.zsazsazsu1963.etsy.com

Wendy Viel
www.etaussi.etsy.com

Index

A

abbreviations 12, 101, 108
accent rugs 31
accents 10, 41
accessories 28, 30–31, 40,
    42, 49–51, 76, 120,
    129–30, 139, 143, 153
acrylic 8, 29, 35, 38, 43
adjusting sizes 110
alpaca 8, 28, 35, 40
alternate (alt) 12
aluminum hooks 23
analogous colors 33
angora 8, 28, 35, 40
animal fibers 28, 35, 41, 178
approximately (approx) 12
Aran 9, 15, 31, 34
arm length adjustments 110
armholes 107
around-the-post
    stitches 90–91
art pieces 42
artistic wire 42
asterisks 105–6, 108
Australia 15
avant-garde pieces 42
avoiding pitfalls 106–7

B

baby items 49, 147, 153
baby weight 15, 30
back loop (BL) 12
back loop inserts 70–71
back loop rows 119
back popcorn 120
back post (BP) 12
back post stitches 90–91
backstitch 177

bags 42, 50–51, 94, 129,
    160, 177
ball bands 9, 38, 178
ball winders 10, 36–37
balls 9–10, 36
bamboo hooks 21, 23
bamboo yarn 29, 43
basic shapes 128–41
basic stitches 68–91, 112–27
baskets 42
basketweave 90
beads 50, 154–55, 178
between (bet) 12
blanket stitch 144, 162
blankets 29, 38, 50, 94,
    122, 129, 132, 146
blends 29
blocking 10, 109, 172–73,
    178
bobbles 102, 147
bodices 160
boho chic 49
borders 142–51
both loop inserts 70–71
bouclé 8, 27, 40
bowls 42
breathable yarns 28
bulky yarns 10, 15, 31
bunting 132
bust line circumference
    adjustments 110
buttonholes 49, 149, 158
buttons 49, 149, 158–59,
    178

C

cables 90, 122–23
cakes 10
cardigans 165
care 178
cashmere 8, 28
center pull balls 36–37
centimeter (cm) 12
chains (ch) 9, 12, 14, 59,
    64–66, 84–85, 96, 102,
    148
challenging yarns 40–41
chunky yarn 10, 31, 78
circles 129, 132
circular crochet 130
clingy hooks 21
closed squares 6, 136
clusters 102
coarse yarns 8
cobweb yarns 9, 15
coffee pot cozies 51
color wheel 33
comfort grip hooks 21, 23
complementary colors 33
continue (cont) 12
continuous rounds 48
contrasting color (CC) 12
conversions 14–15, 22
cool colors 33
cords 51, 160–61
corners 148
cotton 21, 28–29, 35, 155
counting chains 66–67
cowls 176
cozies 51, 120
crab stitch 146
craft yarn 15
crocheted joins 174–75

cushion covers 50–51, 94,
122, 176
customizing patterns 110
cutting tools 46

D
darning needles 47
decrease (dec) 10, 12, 110,
130–31
dense fabrics 26, 28
double crochet (dc) 12, 14,
69, 76–77, 85, 88, 90–91,
99, 116–17, 130
double crochet together
(dc2tog) 12
double knitting (DK) 9, 15,
30, 34
double triple (dtr) 12, 85
drape 30, 43, 74, 78
drawstrings 51, 160–61
dye lots 9, 38

E
edges/edgings 41, 49–51, 66,
117, 142–51, 160, 172
elasticity 29, 35
embellishments 49–51, 129,
143, 152–67, 178
embroidered edgings 144
embroidery scissors 46
end-of-row problems 83
environmentally friendly
hooks 21
estimated usage 38
Europe 6, 14–15, 22, 69
even 102
extras 44–55
eyelash yarn 41

F
fabric 42, 94
fabric density 34–35, 72,
94, 114–23, 150
fast hooks 21
fastening off 102, 105,
170–71
feel 43
felted projects 26
felting 178
fiber content 28–29
fiber types 35, 43
finger length adjustments
110
fingering 15, 30
finishing 168–79
fisherman yarn 15
flat buttons 158
flat shapes 129, 132–38
flax 28
flowers 134
flowery squares 137
fluff 11
following (foll) 12
foot length adjustments 110
foundation chains 9, 64–66,
102
fringes 50, 162–63
front loop (FL) 12, 119
front loop inserts 70–71
front popcorn 120
front post (FP) 12, 90–91
fun fur yarn 41

G
galleries 52–57, 124–27
garments 10, 28, 30–31,
38, 40, 48–50, 74, 76,
109–10, 115, 122,
129–30, 143, 147, 153,
160, 176
gauge 8, 10, 14, 46, 72,
83, 93–96, 109
gauge swatches 40, 46,
92–99, 110
getting lost 107–8
gift items 178
gloves 110
goats 8, 40
gram (g) 12
granny squares 6, 76,
104–5, 133
granny triangles 135

H
half double crochet (hdc) 12,
14, 74–75, 85, 115
half stitches 99
hand sewing needles 47
hand washing 49
handbags 50–51
handles 21
hanks 9, 36
hats 51, 94, 97, 110,
139, 176
hearts 138
hemp 28, 51
hexagons 129–30, 132,
134
highlighting 107, 109
hip size adjustments 110
holding yarn 10

home goods/household
items 28, 30–31, 38, 42,
76, 122, 143
hoods 51, 160
hook gauge 9, 47
hook holds 59–60
hook sizes 22–23, 38
hook types 20–21
hooks 8, 18–23
hourglass shapes 6, 140

I

imperial measurements
14
inch (in) 12
increase (inc) 10, 12, 110,
130–31
inserting into chain/stitch
70–71
instructions 104–7
internal pockets 151
ironing 172

J
jewelry 42
joining 9, 174–77

K
knife hold 60
knitted goods 144
knitting needles 38

L
lace projects 9, 28, 30, 49,
118, 144, 172
laceweight 8–9, 15, 30
lambswool 35
large projects 29, 38

laundering 38, 49–50, 153,
158, 170, 178
leather 42, 51
left handed holds 60
lengthening 110
light fingering 15
light worsted 15
lightweight 30
linen 28
lips 20–21, 23
loftiness 29
look 43
loop (lp) 12
loop stitch 86–87

M

machine-washable items
29, 49
maintenance 178
manmade fibers 29
mattress stitch 176
measurements 14, 97–99,
109–10
measuring tools 46
medallions 10
memory 172
merino 8, 29, 43
mesh stitch 118
metal hooks 21
metallic yarn 41
meter (m) 12
meterage 9
metric measurements 14, 22
microfiber 29
millimeter (mm) 12
mohair 8, 28–29, 35, 40
moth control 178
motifs 10

N
necks 20, 35
needle gauge 9
New Zealand 15
non-separating zippers 50
notions 44–55
novelty yarns 21, 41
nylon 29

O
one-way separating
zippers 50
ounce (oz) 12
ovals 136

P
paper yarn 42
parentheses 105–6, 108
patch pockets 150, 176
pattern instructions 94, 96,
99, 104–7
pattern (patt) 12
pattern reading 100–111
pencil hold 60
picot 10, 145–46
pilling 11, 26
pitfalls 106–7
place markers (pm) 12
plant fibers 28, 35, 41
plastic hooks 21, 23
plied yarn 8, 26
pockets 150–51, 176
polar weight 15
polyester 29
pompoms 51, 156–57
popcorn stitch 102,
120–21
posts 10

pot holders 28, 120
pressing cloths 172
prestrung beads 155
previous (prev) 12
puckering 88
pulling yarn 36–37
purses 50

R
rabbits 8, 40
raffia 42
rayon 28
reading patterns 100–111
remaining (rem) 12
repeat (rep) 12, 105–6, 108
ribbing 90
ribbon yarn 41
ribbons 178
right handed holds 60
right side (RS) 10, 12, 48, 102, 174
round (rnd) 12
roving weight 15
row gauge 10, 94, 97–98
rug yarn 10, 15, 31
rugs 31, 42, 86
rulers 46

S
safety pins 48
sandpaper 21
scarves 51, 78, 94, 120
schematics 10, 109, 172
scissors 46
seaming 172
self adhesive notes 107
semicircles 135

sequins 50, 154–55, 178
sew through buttons 49
sewing machines 164
sewn joins 174–75
shank buttons 49, 158
shank of hooks 20
shapes 128–41
shaping 35, 110, 160
shawls 94, 118, 122
shell with picot 145
shells 8, 102, 117, 145
shortening 110
shoulder length adjustments 110
shoulder seams 177
shrinking 26, 116
silk 28–29
single crochet join 174–75
single crochet (sc) 12, 14, 48, 72–73, 84–86, 99, 114, 117, 130–31, 141, 145, 148
single crochet two together (sc2tog) 12
single ply 8, 26
sizing 109–10, 172
skeins 9–10, 36–37
skip (sk) 12, 14, 102
skirt length adjustments 110
skirts 110
slip stitch 12, 82–83, 104
slip stitch join 174–75
slip knots 62–63
slippery hooks 23
slub 11
small hearts 138
socks 30, 110, 139
soft furnishings 49–50

soft yarns 8
space (sp) 12
spheres 6, 129–30, 139
spike stitch 88–89
splitty yarn 23, 26, 41
sports yarn 15
square brackets 108–9
squares 129, 132, 136–37
steaming 10, 172
steel hooks 21
stitch conversions 14–15
stitch definition 43
stitch gauge 10, 94, 97
stitch markers 48, 141
stitch patterns 112–27
stitch (st) 12
straight 102
straight rulers 46
stripes 41
super-bulky yarn 10, 15, 31
suppliers 38
swatches 10, 40, 46, 92–99, 110
sweaters 30, 50, 94, 107, 109–10
swifts 10, 37
synthetic yarn 8, 29, 35, 38, 43, 172

T
tails of yarn 62–63
taller stitches 80–81
tapes 46
tassels 50, 166, 178
tea cozies 51, 120
tension 8–10, 14, 46, 61, 66, 72, 74, 76, 83, 88, 91, 94, 96–97, 109, 172

terms 8–11, 14, 69, 101–2, 104
texture 27, 40–41, 90, 120
thread 9, 15, 21
three dimensional projects 48, 90, 120, 129, 139–41
through back loop (tbl) 12
tips 27, 38, 40, 48–49, 66, 70, 72, 74, 76, 78, 80, 82, 84, 86, 88, 96–98, 116–17, 120, 122, 150, 155, 166, 177–78
together (tog) 12
tones 33
tools 46–48
torso length adjustments 110
toys 6, 30, 72, 129, 139
triangles 130, 132
trims 44–55, 147, 152–67
triple (tr) 12, 78–79, 85
triple triple (trtr) 12
troubleshooting 23, 43, 67, 83, 99, 106–7, 138, 141, 147–49, 151, 155
tubes 6, 129–30, 139, 141
turning chains 9, 83–85, 102
two-way separating zippers 50

U
United Kingdom (UK) 9, 14–15, 22, 30
United States (US) 6, 9, 14–15, 22, 30–31, 69

W
waistline adjustments 110
warm colors 33
washcloths 28
washing 29, 172
weaving ends 9, 170–71
weight 9, 14–15, 27, 30–31, 34, 43
whip stitch 161–62, 165, 176
winding by hand 37
wool 8, 28–29, 35, 51, 178
working loop 9, 66, 82
working yarn 9
worsted 9, 15, 31
woven goods 144
wraps 122
wrong side (WS) 10, 12, 48, 102, 174

Y
yardage 9
yarn ball bands 9, 38–39, 178
yarn care 178
yarn color 32–33, 38, 40, 43, 88
yarn holds 59, 61
yarn needles 9, 47
yarn over (yo) 12, 14
yarn substitutions 34–35
yarn types 26–27
yarn weight 9, 14–15, 27, 30–31, 34, 43
yarns 24–43

Z
zipper foot 164
zippers 50–51, 164–65

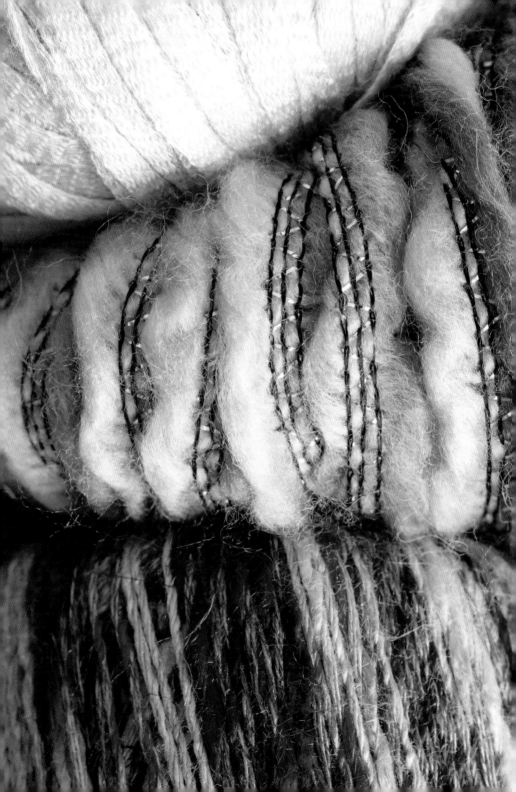

Acknowledgments

I am very grateful to all those who made this book possible.
Isheeta Mustafi at RotoVision was a true ally throughout
the process and it was a real pleasure to work with her.
Jane Roe and Tamsin Richardson were a great help and
I am so thankful. Michael Wicks' beautiful photography
and Sarah Lawrence's brilliant illustrations made the book
look terrific; thank you. Emma Atkinson and Lucy Smith's
great page design brought everything together.

And finally, I can never thank my wonderful husband, Julian,
enough for the patience and encouragement he always
provides; lots of love from your madly-crocheting wife!

35674056625892